The Sisterhood of the Enchanted Forest

THE

SISTERHOOD

OF THE

ENCHANTED FOREST

Sustenance, Wisdom, and Awakening
in Finland's Karelia

NAOMI MORIYAMA
& WILLIAM DOYLE

PEGASUS BOOKS
NEW YORK LONDON

THE SISTERHOOD OF THE ENCHANTED FOREST

Pegasus Books, Ltd.
148 West 37th Street, 13th Floor
New York, NY 10018

Copyright © 2021 by Naomi Moriyama & William Doyle

First Pegasus Books cloth edition October 2021

Interior design by Rachel Reiss

"The Realm of the Enchanted Forest" map illustrated by
Lara Andrea Taber | 2design art co.

ISBN: 978-1-64313-646-2

10 9 8 7 6 5 4 3 2 1

Printed in the United States of America
Distributed by Simon & Schuster
www.pegasusbooks.com

This book discusses foraging for mushrooms and other foods in nature. While these can
be deeply rewarding and fulfilling experiences, please exercise care and only consume
those foods you can positively identify and confirm are 100% safe.

This book is intended to provide helpful and informative information on the subjects
addressed. It is sold with the understanding that the authors and publisher are not
engaged in rendering medical, health, or any other kind of personal professional services
in the book. The reader should consult her or his medical, health, or other competent
professional before adopting any of the ideas in this book or drawing inferences from
them. The authors and publisher specifically disclaim all responsibility for any liability,
loss, or risk, personal or otherwise, which is incurred as a consequence, directly or
indirectly, of the use and application of any of the contents of this book.

This book is dedicated to our son.

Contents

The Realm
of the
Enchanted
Forest

The Land
of Women –
possible location of
Terra Feminarum

Lake
Pielinen

• Temple of the
Forest - Paateri

• The Sacred
Mountain - Koli

Berry Fields of
Kinahmo

Kolvananuuro
Gorge

North
Karelia

Joensuu –
Capital of
the Forest

Ilomantsi –
The House on the
Edge of Forever

• Island
of Joy

Russia ▷

Artic Circle

Lakeland –
Savonlinna
Punkaharju

Mushroom Fields
of Kesälahti

Finland

Helsinki

Not to exact scale

What is this fragrance around me?
What is this quietness?
What is this knowledge of peace in my heart?
What strange, great, new thing is this?
I can hear the flowers growing
and the talk of the trees in the wood.
I think all my old dreams are ripening,
all the hopes and the wishes I sowed.
Everything's quiet around me,
Everything's gentle and sweet.
Great flowers are opening up in my heart
with a fragrance of deepest peace.

—EINO LEINO, *PEACE*

Wide-spread they stand, the Northland's dusky forests,
Ancient, mysterious, brooding savage dreams;
Within them dwells the Forest's mighty God,
And wood-sprites in the gloom weave magic secrets.

—JEAN SIBELIUS, *TAPIOLA*

The Sisterhood of the Enchanted Forest

The Enchanted Forest

I CLOSE MY EYES—AND I am in the forest.

I am walking on a soft carpet of needles and moss, in a wilderness of birch, spruce, and pine trees.

I am drenched in pure, otherworldly silence, and my lungs are caressed by the cleanest air on the planet.

It is Nordic high summer here in the remote forest of Karelia in Finland, but the trees are so tall and their vegetation is so thick that only occasional shafts of sunlight pierce the fairy landscape.

I am on the edge of the Western world—to the east are the endless forests of the desolate Russian taiga; to the north is a sliver of Norway and the Arctic Ocean.

I am traveling in a vast cathedral of nature, in the largest national forest in Europe. I am alone but not lonely, and I am perfectly safe. This is a life-altering realm of tranquility, peace, and beauty, a forest that has inspired and nourished my soul, and transformed my life.

I am traveling in the happiest, greenest, and safest nation in the world, the country with the world's cleanest water and the best public schools, a country where parenthood is championed by law, childhood is revered, schoolchildren are required by the government to play outdoors three or four times a day, and long-distance trains contain mini playgrounds and mini libraries for children to enjoy.

Six years ago I moved here with my family for six months, to the great forest of Karelia, a romantic and mysterious region that helped inspire J. R. R. Tolkien's Middle-earth fantasies.

In the forest I found something that changed my life.

I discovered a tribe of invincible women—and they became my soul sisters.

This is the story of how I discovered an enchanted forest in a place not far from the Arctic Circle. In Finland, I found a land of unspoiled nature, a culinary symphony of succulent wild edibles, herbs, berries, mushrooms, and fish, all harvested by hand from the pristine forest, rivers, and lakes. I found an entire nation of people who roam the woods and forage for the earth's treasures, incorporate them into traditional dishes and beverages, and preserve them for long, dark winters.

This is the nation that is ranked as the number one top contributor to humanity per capita—where gender equality and women's political and social rights are baked into not only the nation's one-hundred-year-old founding constitution, but into everyday practice, offering inspiration to the world.

It is a nation with its share of social problems, including racism and domestic violence, but it is also a nation that leads the world in striving to achieve a better life for all its citizens. In 2021, Finland ranked first among the world's 160 nations in sustainable development, according to a United Nations report, which found that Finland had achieved or nearly achieved the UN's goals on alleviating poverty, improving health, education, water, energy, peace, the rule of law, and reducing inequality.

This is a nation that today is run by women—the thirty-four-year-old prime minister is a new mother who leads a governing coalition of five parties, all of which are all led by women.

I lived here once. I came in the summertime. As an idyllic summer and fall gave way to a subarctic winter of mind-bending darkness and cold, I faced my hopes, my fears, and my future. Over the course of six unforgettable months, I found my life transformed, and I discovered the power that lay within me—with the inspiration of my "sisters of the forest."

Then I tried to leave.

But I kept coming back.

What would happen if you built one of the world's most advanced societies inside a forest, and strove to make women full partners in power? You would have Finland—a place that actually exists in the world right now.

This book is the story of how I fell in love with Finland and the story of how its women, its society, and its nature have astonished and inspired me.

This is the story of glimpses my family and I had of this strange, beautiful, and faraway land when we lived there as residents and visitors from New York City in 2015, 2016, and 2017, and then returned to as residents in 2020 and 2021.

Come with me, let's take a journey deep into one of Europe's last great wildernesses, and join the sisterhood of the enchanted forest.

A Promise

In the midst of winter, I finally learned that there was in me an invincible summer.

—ALBERT CAMUS

IT BEGAN WITH A PROMISE in springtime.

Several years ago, my husband, William, got the news that he had been selected as a Fulbright Scholar to study and write about the world-renowned Finnish public school system, and to lecture to university graduate students about his career specialties in the media and publishing businesses.

We were going to move from Manhattan to Finland with our seven-year-old son. I was a full-time stay-at-home parent at the time.

I knew almost nothing of Finland, except that it was somewhere in the Nordic region atop Europe, and it was supposed to have great schools. By now, I had pretty much forgotten about my husband's applying for the Fulbright Scholar program many months ago. It seemed like a fun idea at the time, but I had a lot of other things to think about. Then, I realized that Finland was to be my new home. I plunged into online research, and borrowed books from the library.

The more I read, the more I worried.

I was going to live for six months in a far-off place, in the most sparsely populated country in the European Union.

Finland? I thought. *He couldn't have picked a country like Italy, France, or Australia—somewhere I'd actually like to go? This does not look good at all.*

I'd spent most of my life in the high-energy, ultra-populated metropolises of Tokyo and New York City, where I had plenty of friends and things to do. But according to the few books and articles I could find, Finland seemed like a dark, cold, and lonely place. We would be living not in Finland's sleek, cosmopolitan capital, Helsinki, but in Joensuu, home to the University of Eastern Finland, where William's project was based.

A friend introduced me to Jaana, a Finnish-American medical doctor who had lived in New York for many years. She is president of the Finland Center Foundation and founder of the Kota Alliance, a nonprofit that focuses on women's rights and gender equality, and she reputedly knew practically every Finn who lived in New York City. She was very helpful in filling me in on Finland—but she had never been to Joensuu, and didn't know anybody who lived there.

Joensuu, I learned, is the provincial capital of a remote part of rural Finland called North Karelia, a forest-and-lake district right on the Russian border, and is the easternmost municipality in the continental European Union. The city was founded by Tsar Nicholas I in 1848 when Finland was part of Russia, and the city is as close to St. Petersburg as it is to Helsinki.

I was headed, in other words, to the absolute edge of the Western world.

According to the articles and books I read, the people of Finland were very smart, reliable, trustworthy, honest, and hardworking, but they also were reportedly shy, modest, and reserved, fond of silence, and averse to small talk and chit-chat. A standard joke was, "How can you spot a Finnish extrovert?" The punch line: "In the elevator, he's the guy who stares at someone else's shoes instead of his own."

Another joke was about a Finnish wife who complained to her husband, "I hear Italian and French and American husbands tell their wives how much they love them. Why don't you ever tell me you love me?" Her husband mumbled, "Do you remember the day we were married, when I told you I loved you?" "Yes," recalled the wife. "If I change my mind," said the husband, "I'll let you know."

Then there was the story of the gruff Helsinki taxi driver who picked up a fare at a hotel during an international soccer match. During the ride, his American customer noted, "I saw the players from Northern Ireland at breakfast this morning. They looked sad. Did they lose the match?"

"No," deadpanned the unsmiling Finnish taxi driver, without missing a beat. "They are sad because they are in Finland."

It seemed that periods of detached, mordant sadness were a character requirement for the Finns. The famed Finnish

artist Hugo Simberg, for example, created a series of paint-
ings starring a favorite character, Death, in a variety of col-
orful activities. They included *The Peasant and Death at the
Gates of Heaven and Hell, Death and the Potato Peeler,* and *The
Garden of Death.* In his painting *Playmates,* the skeleton form
of Death smiles down at a pair of innocent children, and in
The Wounded Angel, named Finland's national painting by
popular vote in 2006, a pair of boys haul an injured girl-angel
on wooden poles, their faces a portrait of sadness.

Sometimes, these gloomy character descriptions of
taciturn and less-than-slap-happy people sounded like
caricatures of Japanese—my own native tribe, whom I lived
among until I moved to the United States for college. "The
Finns take words seriously, and they don't say anything unless
they have something important to say," I read. *Wait a minute!*
I thought. *"Silence is Golden!" That's my Japanese dad's mantra!*

Pondering the prospect of moving there, I thought, *Well,
maybe I'd be more at home in Finland than my husband, who
spent most of his life in the fast-talking, loud-talking city of New
York. At least I think I know how to read nuances.*

I was at a turning point in my life. I had been a full-time
stay-at-home mother for nearly eight years, and an entrepreneur and corporate marketing executive for twelve years
before that. As our son progressed beyond toddlerhood, I
didn't know what the next chapter of my life would be. To be
honest, I was unsure of reentering the workforce, as I feared
being seen as too old, too overqualified, or too "obsolete" to
land a fulfilling job. Living in a mysterious, far-off land, perhaps I would have time and space to reflect on my future.

The thought of escaping New York for a while was also an appealing one. A distant voice in my head said, *I just want to get away. I just want to take a nice long break from my hectic life of stressing, texting, urban noise, bad news on TV, fragmented streams of images and words on social media, and constant demands for my attention.*

The place where we were headed, the district of North Karelia, about 250 miles northeast of Helsinki, was reportedly a beautiful region of pristine forests, thousands of lakes, rustic charm, sparsely populated villages, and the mystic power of nature. Most of the people spoke English, as did the great majority of Finns, especially younger ones. *Maybe*, I thought, *Finland won't be too bad. It could be the break I need.*

But still, I worried. About cold. About darkness. New York City had plenty of both in wintertime, too. I could barely make it through New York winters, and by March I usually was, like many other New Yorkers, cranky and nearly stir-crazy from being confined indoors with little sunlight and fresh air for four months. It was March in New York, and we had just suffered a nearly-unendurable four solid months of it, but Finland seemed much worse.

I learned on the internet that the sunset in Joensuu was 3:39 P.M. by late autumn, which meant that twilight arrived not long after lunchtime! Winters in Finland were reportedly savagely cold, with temperatures regularly hovering around minus 20 degrees Fahrenheit, and the nation ranked relatively high in depression, suicide, and domestic violence, as many northern populations experience.

The more I read, the more I worried. On top of all this, most of the country looked as flat as a pancake. There seemed to be few hills or real mountains, and very little to break up the visual monotony.

I feared that by November, I'd be lonely and depressed. I imagined trying to make friends with people and being coldly rebuffed. I imagined I would be stuck in an apartment with no one to talk to, nowhere to go, and nothing to do while my husband was at work and my son was at school. I had a pathetic vision of myself sitting at a dining room table plowing through my friends' Facebook pages, desperately trying to connect with a faraway universe that was familiar and friendly. Expecting this, I created a Facebook account so I could stay connected to the outside world.

Adding layers of strangeness to the mix was the fact Finland was a major mystery to everyone, including itself. Finland is considered a Nordic nation, along with Sweden, Norway, Denmark, and Iceland, with whom it shares many social values. But despite the fact that Finland is often grouped with Sweden, Norway, and Denmark as part of Scandinavia named after people of the Scandes Mountains of northern Europe, technically Finland is not Scandinavian, since ethnically and linguistically Finland has surprisingly little in common with the others, and only a tiny portion of the Scandes foothills poke into Finland's extreme northwest. The origins of the Finnish language are shrouded in mystery, and it is related not to northern European languages, but to possible ancient roots in Estonian, Hungarian, and Uralic sources from as far south as central Europe and as far east as the Ural Mountains of interior Russia. The Finns themselves debate exactly where the Finnish language and people came from, but so far no one had fully cracked the mystery.

In the books and articles I could find, these Finns seemed extremely quirky, occasionally to the point of downright weirdness. "Some think the Finns are crazy," wrote Finnish resident Harald Haarmann in his book *Modern Finland*. "One cannot deny that altogether because, in a way, it is true, especially when looking at some rather unusual competitions with which the Finns amuse themselves."

The Finns, I learned, hold a wide range of bizarre competitions, often in the "silly season" of summer, when daylight stretches far into nighttime. The town of Sonkajärvi, for example, hosts the annual international *eukonkanto*, or "wife-carrying," competition, in which men place women over their shoulders and dash across an 833-foot racetrack through rough terrain, featuring two dry obstacles and one water obstacle. The carried woman must weigh a minimum of 108 pounds, and can be a friend or girlfriend, too. The wacky sport apparently was inspired by dark legends of forest-dwelling bandits who stole women from their homes, but the modern event is a delightful experience for both spectators and participants. According to the rules, all contestants must have insurance, and all must enjoy themselves.

Other idiosyncratic Finnish "sports matches" include swamp football, held in the town of Hyrynsalmi, the annual World Cell Phone Throwing Championships in Punkaharju, and competitions in sauna-sitting, mosquito-swatting, table-tapping, milkstool-chucking, hay-mowing, rubber-boot hurling, air guitar, and sitting on an ant nest. In one event at *RautalankaFestarit* (Twangy Guitar Festival) in the municipality of Lahti, the goal is to see who can endure painfully sappy folk music for the longest period of time.

In years past, when Finland was mentioned at all in global affairs, it could be the subject of abject ridicule. In the 2000s, Finnish food was publicly dismissed as awful by the leaders of no less than two fellow European nations—Italian prime minister Silvio Berlusconi and French president Jacques Chirac. Monty Python's 1980 *Contractual Obligation Album* featured an instantly forgettable anthem titled "Finland," which included these less-than-epic lyrics: "Finland, Finland, Finland, Finland has it all, You're so sadly neglected, And often ignored, A poor second to Belgium, When going abroad."

In 1993, CBS aired a downright cruel *60 Minutes* segment titled called "Tango Finlandia," in which star correspondent Morley Safer journeyed to Helsinki to mock elderly Finns dancing sadly and stiffly in community halls, in a country where he said "melancholy, sorrow and shyness abound," and people were "grimly in touch with no one but themselves." The report noted, "It's no surprise that Finland has one of the lowest birthrates and one of the highest suicide rates."

What Safer didn't know was that at that very moment, during one of the worst recessions in national memory, Finland was in the process of building itself into global leadership in the mobile phone market through local company Nokia, which peaked in the 2000s before losing out to Apple; and in childhood education, when in 2000, to everyone's surprise, including the Finns, the nation ranked number one in the world in international benchmark math, science, and reading scores. Today, Finland continues to score near the top of European nations, and is number one among industrialized nations for the equity and efficiency of its schools and the well-being of its students.

I did notice some intriguing attractions to Finland, at least on paper. Despite its reputation as a freezing, dark, tight-lipped, and even quirky nation, Finland was in the process of collecting a wall full of gold medals in a wide variety of international rankings. Later, these rankings would include, confusingly for such an allegedly morose people, the number one spot in the United Nations' "World's Happiest Nation" index for four years, running through 2021.

This country of fewer than six million people, barely a century old, which had much of its territory above the Arctic Circle, somehow was being ranked the number one nation in the world or the European Union—or a close second or third, usually to a fellow Nordic nation—for stability, personal freedom and choice, human well-being, rule of law, prosperity, trust, gender equality, upward social mobility, safety, ease of starting a business, governance, social justice, human capital, quality of life, life satisfaction, literacy, human rights, least corruption, lowest poverty, lowest maternal and child mortality, election integrity, best schools, strongest banks, best police and internal security, strongest courts, cleanest air, and cleanest food and water.

The Finnish health care system was said to be excellent. The social welfare system, including generous parental leave for both mothers and fathers, was reportedly so good that

Finnish fathers are the only men worldwide who spend more time with their children than women. According to the law, all Finnish children under the formal school-starting age of seven have the right to high-quality early childhood education and care, and since 1943, free school lunches have been offered to all children.

Finland, I learned, was ranked one of the best nations to be a mother, a child, or a girl or woman, and one of the best nations for gender equality. It had the most female members of Parliament in Europe, the world's number one ranking for educational attainment for women, and was the first nation to offer full rights for women to vote and run for office, dating back to 1906. Today, it consistently ranks at the very top of nations for women's rights and women's equality. Finland had a female president from 2000 to 2012, a period in which Finland also had two female prime ministers, five female speakers of Parliament, and the world's highest share of female cabinet ministers. Finland is so supportive of gender equality that it has a campaign to build global enthusiasm for gender-neutral pronouns—there is no *he* or *she* in Finnish, only *hän*, which covers everyone.

I grew up in Japan, where women are often still expected to walk several steps behind their husbands, and I'd lived much of my adult life in the United States, where the headlines were soon dominated by a tidal wave of #MeToo scandals. In Finland, however, I read that great strides had been made toward gender equality, and in some rankings, Finland was leading the world in gender progress. For that reason alone I thought Finland might be a great place to expose our child to.

In three rankings that really caught my attention, Finland was named the number one nation for expatriates with families, with the best public schools for children, and the biggest national forest in Europe, accounting for around 70 percent of the country's surface area. Technically, Sweden has more trees, but they cover a smaller percentage of the nation. The Finns "are a forest people at heart," wrote author Deborah Swallow in her book *CultureShock! Finland: A Survival Guide to Customs and Etiquette.* "One of their core beliefs is about looking after the environment. Laws, dating back to 1886, promote well-managed, sustainable forestry and these are updated constantly with new and pertinent regulations. This is just one incidence of how long the Finns have been 'green' in their outlook." She added, "To a large extent, their climate, nature and geography has shaped the Finnish mindset. They perceive themselves at a distance from other cultures, apart and separate—but inextricably mixed with their forests and lakes."

Compared with the rest of the world, Finland, it seemed, was a highly advanced, family-friendly forest nation, with an inspiring record of achievement in social services and gender equality, relative to most of the rest of the world. "Of course, Finland is not Utopia," Danny Dorling and Annika Koljonen would write in their 2020 book *Finntopia,* "but today it offers one of the closest approximations," and "its people have worked to build a better world with far more rigor and determination than any other nation on the planet."

Despite these tantalizing plusses, I told my husband that based on my reading, there seemed to be a high probability that by mid-October, when the shroud of freezing darkness slammed down on Finland, I would be miserable.

I needed the option to come back to New York in October if I really wanted to. We struck a deal.

We promised each other that if I hated Finland, I could bail out and I'd see him and our son back in New York around New Year's, when his university assignment was over. Relief!

In the middle of summer, we boarded a flight to Finland.

The Professor's Welcome

The forest has been the mainstay of the life of all the Finnic peoples. The forest was governed by a life-sustaining mother who in Finnish folk incantations ultimately inherited the role of the Virgin Mary. The forest is approached with respect, but timidly: man is a guest, who does not have any self-evident rights over the forest.

—JUHA PENTIKÄINEN

WE LANDED AT THE WORLD's loneliest airport.

An hour-long propeller-plane shuttle flight from Helsinki deposited us at Joensuu Airport, which from the air looked like much else in Finland—a clearing carved out of a thick forest of pine, spruce, and silver-white birch trees, a land-scape sprinkled with lakes, pastures, and fields, little wooden houses, and the occasional two-lane road.

There were no other planes visible, and the single-room airport featured one gate, one luggage carousel, and a single waiting taxi. The midsummer air was bracingly clean and crisp, laced with a rich, hypnotic pine fragrance.

"Welcome to Finland!" exclaimed a youthful woman with reddish-brown hair who gave us a huge warm smile and a bear hug. She was Helmi Järviluoma-Mäkelä, a humanities professor at the University of Eastern Finland, and William's faculty host and sponsor.

Helmi was the first local Finnish person I met, and she was beaming with joy and conversation, which from my reading was not what I was expecting from a Finn. There was no awkward silence. She was a highly accomplished humanities professor, a globally renowned authority and researcher on soundscapes, and a new grandmother, and she exuded humor, professorial curiosity, intellectual passion, and enthusiasm about pretty much everything.

In 2019, Helmi would be named the number one best professor in all of Finland by her peers, and it wasn't hard to see why. She turned out to be one of the gentlest, warmest, happiest, most curious, positive, and intellectually out-there people I'd ever come across, and a vivid prelude to many Finns I would encounter, especially Finnish women—who, I soon discovered, are a very special breed of people. "Finnish women are much more outgoing and approachable than the men and often command three or four languages," the *Telegraph* (UK) reported in 2006. "Their position in society and business is well-respected and superior to that of women in most other cultures."

Residents of the district of North Karelia, I soon learned, have a reputation in Finland for being more open, outgoing, and expressive than other Finns, a legacy of its remote, rugged location; its close proximity to the often exuberant and expressive people of Russia; and of the fact that thousands of people on both sides of the border connect their heritage to the Karelian ethnic grouping, which has its own language, and its own identity as a country people who are sturdy, self-reliant, and life-loving. In other parts of Finland, I later learned, the idea of being "forest people" could mean being contemplative and quiet, lest you stir the bears in the forest into anger. But in Karelia, I soon observed that it often seemed like a license to party.

During the twenty-minute drive from the airport to our new apartment near the center of the little city, we chatted nonstop while passing bright green forests and fields, as Helmi pointed out the sights to our family. There was the teacher-training school that our young son would attend on the university campus, a complex of sleek pink-brick Nordic-modern buildings. There were the open-air market stalls of Joensuu's *tori* (marketplace) in the town square, where locals sold berries, fish, vegetables, and handmade crafts. There was a coffee shop where we could have *iltapäiväkahvit* (afternoon coffee) with *korvapuusti* (a cinnamon bun).

There on the side streets of Joensuu were old Russian-style house facades mingling with Euro-modern apartment buildings. There was the beautiful modern library, with a vast collection of children's books, where on a Friday or Saturday night we soon would witness a startling sight—scores of Joensuu residents packing the tables and chairs in standing-room-only fashion, intently and quietly hunched over paper books, newspapers, and magazines. Finland is the most literate nation in the world, with the most ardent readers, and they take their libraries very seriously.

Shafts of brilliant, midsummer sun filtered through the towering birch trees that flanked the main streets of Joensuu. As Helmi drove us around on a tour, I was amazed to see that in many areas the thick forest seemed to weave and dance gracefully all around and right into the city. The city planners had left much of the forest intact when they carved out Joensuu, giving it the fairy-tale illusion of a lumberjack town in Colorado, or an Alpine valley town, oddly punctuated with a phalanx of lumpy Soviet–style office and department store buildings that formed the town center, or *keskusta*.

I soon learned that in a stroke of genius, the city planners of Joensuu, as is typical in Finland, allowed the forest to dominate much of the city, and the connections between neighborhoods often consisted of gentle pathways through unspoiled treescapes, perfect for biking and walking—and cross-country skiing in the winter. If you power walked for fifteen minutes in most directions, you'd be in the forest. Bike lanes and bike paths, it seemed, were everywhere, and highly popular. Joensuu is the forest research capital of Europe, since it is the headquarters of the European Forest Institute, a multinational, nongovernmental organization nestled in a stunning wooden building on the campus of the University of Eastern Finland.

Near the lakefront we saw a neighborhood containing scores of tiny, packed-together, multicolored Nordic–style wooden houses with micro gardens and footpaths that led to a communal shower and sauna. Each was of an entirely different design. I'd never seen anything like it other than in illustrated children's fairytales. Helmi explained they were *kesämökki*, or cozy little summer cottages for people who lived in the area, perfect for relaxing, having a swim or lakeside picnic or boating trip.

Joensuu is the capital of one of the last great wilderness areas of Europe and the easternmost district in the continental European Union, North Karelia, which shares a 192-mile border with Russia and is comprised largely of lakes, farms, and gentle hills, and forests lightly populated by generally shy brown bears, wolverines, and elks.

The city was founded as a logging and trading post in 1845, at the spot where the River Pielisjoki flows into Lake Pyhäselkä. While it is located in the most economically depressed district of Finland, beset with high unemployment, pockets of rural poverty, farm closures, and a struggling timber industry, Joensuu is also home to the University of Eastern Finland, which hosts one of the nation's eight world-leading teacher-training master's degree programs, and a student body drawn not only from Finland but from many European nations, Africa, the Middle East, and Asia.

A visitor from the United Kingdom, *Times* journalist Hilary Finch, described the quiet, stately street where our apartment was located: "The longest, straightest avenue, the Kirkkokatu (Church Street), displays the town's ecclesiastical polarity, with the spire of the red-brick Lutheran church at one end saluting the green and white timbered Orthodox at the other, camouflaged among the ubiquitous silver birches." She added, "It is a town for walking; along the Rantakatu (Shore Street), rafts of logs float downstream to the left, and the immaculately restored pastel-timbered merchants' houses of the 19th century line up on the right. Where the estuary curves into the lake shore and the damp air of the marshy birch woods is heavy with the scent of wild lily of the valley, the Vainoniemi Villa stands like a stage-set for a Chekhov play. A little further on is a massive new open-air stadium; for Joensuu, like any sizeable Finnish town, celebrates the long light days of its short summer with festivals of music, song and street theatre."

The mixture of Russian and Scandinavian themes was typical of Finnish history—before its independence in 1917, Finland was conquered and dominated in turn by the Swedish and Russian Empires. Finland was ruled by Sweden for some six hundred years, leaving behind a strong imprint in the national memory—today Swedish is the nation's second official language. The Russian and Swedish experiences led, some thought, to a certain cultural reluctance by Finns to stand out and "stick one's head up," lest it be swatted down by the colonial oppressor—and a stoic determination to persevere through brutal trials of weather and history, a trait the Finns call *sisu*.

In truth, the Russian period of domination, 1809–1917, when Finland was an autonomous Grand Duchy of the Tsar, was a fairly "soft" occupation until the end, when the Russians tried to oppress and over-Russify Finland, and the Finns endured a bloody "White-Red" civil war that followed Finland's full independence on December 6, 1917. The big border clash with the Soviet Union came in two epic conflicts that unfolded from 1939 through 1944—the Winter War and the Continuation War—and saw the desperate Finns enter a de facto alliance with Nazi Germany to escape total annihilation by the Soviets. Incredibly, the vastly outnumbered Finns, often on skis, outfought the Soviet Army to a standstill, in temperatures that plunged to mind-bending lows.

Much of the fighting raged over this shared ancestral forest land of Karelia, and over four hundred thousand Finns became refugees—not once, but twice. First, they marched west after evacuating their farms and homesteads when large parts of Finnish Karelia were conquered by the Soviets in 1940, then they marched all the way back east to resettle a huge, expanded "Greater Karelia" that was occupied by Finland and pushed the border hundreds of miles east and deep into Russia. Then, they had to evacuate back west to Finland less than three years later, when the Soviets reconquered the region, compelled the Finns to force the Nazis off their territory, and chopped off substantial slices of Finland as part of the armistice settlement. In the process, Finland lost 10 percent of its territory, 30 percent of its energy sources, 22 percent of its forests, and 20 percent of its railway lines, as well as its small Arctic Ocean coastline and much of Karelia, including what had been Finland's second largest city, Viipuri, now called Vyborg by the Russians. In 1952, the same year that Helsinki hosted the Summer Olympics, Finland impressed the world by fully repaying its huge war reparations when the last trainload of reparation goods departed for the Soviet Union.

Even though many Finns today rarely visit remote Joensuu, or just pass through on the road to the hilly Koli National Park, the Karelian region forms a crucial part of the Finnish soul. The mystical landscapes of Koli and Karelia served as inspiration for artists, writers, and composers during the "Golden Age" of romantic, nationalistic art that blossomed in Finland in the 1890s, and often celebrated a classic piece of mid-century Finnish literature called the *Kalevala*.

The *Kalevala* (Land of Heroes), first published in 1835 and then expanded in 1849, was assembled by the Finnish doctor Elias Lönnrot, who wandered throughout Karelia and regions north and east of it, including vast areas now controlled by Russia, collecting local legends, folk tales, poems, and songs. The *Kalevala* became a foundational national document and Finland's most famous literary work, considered by some to be one of the world's great national epics of literature, along with works like the *Illiad* of Greece, the *Nibelungenlied* of Germany, and the *Mahabharata* of India. "We know that, at its publication, the *Kalevala* was seen—and is to a certain extent still seen—as a tale of an ancient Golden Age, when people were better than they are today, when people had closer ties with nature," wrote Emil Nestor Setälä, a Finnish government official and chief author of the Finnish Declaration of Independence, "a time when harmony and a trust in spiritual powers, and above all in the power of the word, prevailed."

The storyline of the *Kalevala* featured a quest for the Sampo, a mysterious magical artifact that confers wealth and good fortune to whoever holds it. The Sampo is sought after, stolen, fought over, and lost, and is described as a mill that produces money, flour, and salt. As a symbol, it resembles other mythical talismans, like the Greek Cornucopia, the Holy Grail of Arthurian legend, and the world tree or tree of life tales common to many cultures.

The *Kalevala* helped inspire *The Hobbit* and *The Lord of the Rings* by J. R. R. Tolkien, who discovered the epic poem as a young man and was so entranced that he studied Finnish so he could read the original, even though he never got to visit Finland. Tolkien recalled that when he began savoring the strange Finnish language, "It was like discovering a wine-cellar filled with bottles of amazing wine of a kind and flavor never tasted before. It quite intoxicated me." A number of themes in the *Kalevala* reappeared in Tolkien's fantasy worlds, including the quest for a powerful magical object, collisions between light and darkness and good and evil, sex and battles between siblings, and orphan heroes setting out on quests through the wilderness.

Karelia was, in fact, the original Middle-earth.

And now it was my home.

My Long-Lost Sisters

As Professor Helmi helped us get squared away in our new apartment, I told her that one of the things I hoped to do while in Joensuu was to learn about regional traditional cuisines. Food is a great interest of mine, and my mother, Chizuko, in Tokyo is such a queen of Japanese home cooking that I wrote three books about it with William, in honor of her and all the people who cook for their loved ones around the world. I thought that learning about local food would be a good way to get to know Finland and Karelia.

Helmi suggested that a great place to start was the outdoor Martha Café in the city square, which during these warm summer months served handmade *karjalanpiirakka* (Karelian pastries) and other iconic local foods. She added that they made them right there in the square.

Helmi explained that "Martha" was a national association of Finnish volunteers who provided social services and support to the community. Members of the association

were called Marthas. The group took its name from the bib-
lical figure of Martha, the aunt of Jesus Christ on his mother
Mary's side, who busily prepared food and laid the table when
Jesus came to visit them. The group's symbol is a billowing
apron. Helmi told me there was a storefront Martha office and
kitchen on the town square that was the organizations' provincial headquarters for North Karelia, and they held cooking
classes there.

Later that day, I sat with my husband and son at a table outside the Martha Café, under a red-and-white striped awning
and a crisp, gorgeous blue sky with small puffy white clouds—
the two colors of the Finnish flag—and sunk my teeth into a
karjalanpiirakka.

It was a scrumptious four-inch-long, three-inch-wide oval-
shaped open pastry with white, rice-porridge filling in the
middle. The pinched rye-flour crust was thin, earthy, and
crunchy, and the filling was super soft and a bit salty—just
the perfect amount of saltiness. It was served with butter and
chopped boiled eggs.

Karjalanpiirakka are to the Finns what bagels are to New
Yorkers, rice balls are to the Japanese, and croissants are to
the French—a simple, mouthwatering savory snack. They are
pretty much everywhere in the North Karelia region and in
Finland—at cafés, gatherings, parties, picnics, and hikes.

It was a crisp, gorgeous summer day of 60 degrees Fahrenheit. The locals complained of an unusually rainy summer,
but the weather lately turned spectacularly beautiful. The
town square was packed with families enjoying late summer
in the brilliant sun.

In a local activity guide, I saw a parent-child baking class offered by the North Karelia Martha Organization in the town square next day, but unfortunately missed it because we were busy settling in. I made a mental note to investigate similar opportunities. A few days later, my husband started work at the university, and our son started class at an English-speaking neighborhood public school, both of which, like so many places in Karelia, were enveloped by the forest.

I checked out the North Karelia Martha website, but couldn't make much sense of it, as it was all in Finnish. I emailed the organization, asking if there were cooking classes for regional and traditional dishes that were offered in English, and added a bit of my background. Katja Kolehmainen, the executive director of the North Karelia Martha chapter, responded immediately, inviting me to their offices to meet her and her fellow Marthas. Katja soon became my close friend and "big sister" figure, even though she was much younger than I. With her help, I began to explore my new surroundings.

AT THE APPOINTED time, I buzzed the door to the Martha office on the Joensuu town square.

The place was filled with laughing, busy women and men clustered around a large table in an open test kitchen. They were drinking coffee and conducting a pastry-baking class, pausing to munch on their fluffy creations.

Spotting me, an obvious outsider, the Marthas invited me in. Excited to hear that I was from New York City, they enveloped me in a bubble of welcomes and chatter.

Within minutes, to my amazement, they were treating me like a long-lost sister.

The Martha women were among the most vibrant, cheerful, expressive, friendly, and curious people I'd ever met. They ranged in age from eighteen to eighty and above, many of them had weekday jobs in various professions, some were full-time staff Marthas, but most were volunteer Marthas. I was astonished at how warm their welcome was. When it came to personalities in this part of Finland at least, it seemed my outgoing, joyful new friend Professor Helmi was no exception.

A striking woman in her early twenties introduced herself as Ringa, and said Katja had asked her to tell me about the Martha organization. Ringa led me over to a conference room appointed with folded napkins, elegant multicolored tableware by the Finnish design brand Iittala, and flower vases designed by the famed Finnish architect Alvar Aalto. She offered me sweet pastries while filling my aqua-blue coffee mug, and told me a story.

Ringa was a university student studying to be a professional nutritionist while working at Martha, and like many younger Finns she spoke fluent English. When an English-speaker is present, many Finns effortlessly switch from speaking Finnish to English.

The Martha Organization, explained Ringa, is one of the world's original women's empowerment groups. It was founded in 1899, an era when most of Finland was rural, poor, and still under Russian domination, as a nonprofit home economics organization to promote women's well-being and family quality of life.

The organization was the brainchild of Lucina Hagman, a schoolteacher and peace activist from the Ostrobothnia region of western Finland, who became one of the first female members of Parliament in the world in the Finnish parliamentary election of 1907. Of the original nineteen female members of the Finnish Parliament, which included teachers, seamstresses, housemaids, and journalists, three of them also were Marthas.

In the early days, the Marthas helped lift up their fellow women, who were often in charge of household and family affairs. They helped them with courses in childcare; cooking and housekeeping; handicrafts; raising chickens, cattle, and pigs; establishing kitchen gardens and growing vegetables and fruits; and harvesting berries and mushrooms from the forests. The goal was to help women help their families become financially independent, physically healthy and confident, and productive members of the community. There were no religious or political objectives; the group existed only to help women and families thrive.

In the decades that followed, the Martha Organization expanded into a volunteer force of what today is comprised of over forty thousand women and men in one thousand local chapters around the country. Similar Nordic women's empowerment groups exist in neighboring Norway and Sweden. Often, multiple generations of Finnish women in a single family become Marthas. The Marthas share knowledge of food, cooking, growing produce, gardening, hygiene, budgeting, and running the household.

Today, the mission of the Marthas is to give people self-confidence and skills to take care of themselves and their families; to promote cultural education and civic advocacy work; to help people start their own small businesses; and to lend a hand to anyone in the community who needs help, including men, women, and children. The Marthas work with the National Council of Women of Finland, an umbrella organization for sixty-seven Finnish women's organizations. All told, the council represents a total of some four hundred thousand Finnish women who focus on advancing and promoting women's rights and gender equality. The Martha Organization is open to all: men, women, LGBTQIA, youth, children, immigrants, expats, even tourists and complete novices.

The Marthas, Ringa explained as she poured me a cup of tea, run social programs in Finland to help elderly people with home visits and housework, and help war refugees from the Middle East and elsewhere, in addition to prisoners, unemployed people, substance-abuse addicts, and people with mental challenges. They teach families with young children about childcare and how to make nutritious baby food on a budget. If they hear about an elderly person who is lonely and lacking social connections, they will invite the person into Martha activities to learn new hobbies, meet new people, and do volunteer work of their own.

In recent years, Martha volunteers conducted seminars for newly arrived Middle Eastern refugees on how to shop for groceries in local markets and how to navigate their new community. A Martha delegation had recently traveled to Cameroon to share insights on nutrition, home economics, and entrepreneurship with local women. To finance their operations, the Marthas run cafés and perform cleaning services around Finland.

Ringa was articulate, confident, intelligent, and warm. I soon found these characteristics common in many locals, regardless of age, gender, and occupation, including salespeople at a smartphone retailer, a twenty-year-old horseback riding instructor, a pharmacist at the local *apteekki* (pharmacy), medical doctors, and technicians and administrative staffs at hospitals. They all exuded a sense of assurance that everything was under control.

My new friend Katja Kolehmainen was a warm, energetic woman who had served as manager of a Finnish government refugee center that served migrants and human trafficking victims from all over the world, and had also worked for the Karelia University of Applied Science. Like most Finns, her life was deeply intertwined with nature. "My family are forest people," she told me. "When you have nature as a child, you have it for the rest of your life. Ever since I learned to walk we were fishing, and picking berries and mushrooms. My father hunted so much that I once complained to him, *Dad, I've had enough rabbits. I want 'real' meat from the supermarket—in a package! With a label!* I find it normal and relaxing and comfortable when I am in woods and the wilderness. I'm not afraid there. I feel I am in my home."

Katja added, "The Martha Organization values are the same today as they were at the time of its foundation in 1899, while specific problems we face are different. Martha teaches people who do not have the skills how to survive and thrive in life. A centerpiece of our work is food—how to make, grow, afford, serve, enjoy, and share it, how to make it healthy and delicious, and how to sell it to supplement family incomes. Food intelligence is essential to one's well-being." This struck a special chord with me, as I had spent much time exploring the healthy food intelligence of traditional Japanese home cooking. Katja added, "Knowing how to grocery shop helps people save money, and how to cook nutritious meals at home helps them be healthy, energetic, and productive. Martha teaches how to clean a house so people live a healthy life. We also teach financial management."

Katja noted proudly, "The Finnish government knows Martha has proven successful methods, and retains us to run courses for different segments in the society: unemployed, post-prison, refugees, people with illness such as diabetes or cancer. Gaining the basic home economics and life skills gives people who might feel lost, for example, those with mental illnesses, a sense of confidence. They feel, 'I can manage,' and they learn to take care of themselves." Today, the group also includes two thousand male members, along with chapters at most Finnish universities. In North Karelia, I would often hear of grandmothers, mothers, and daughters who were all proud Marthas.

Marianne Heikkilä is the Helsinki-based secretary general of the national Martha Organization, in addition to being an ordained Lutheran pastor. She once explained that "when you humble yourself and admit that you are not as independent as you imagined, you will eventually find something better than self-empowerment—a mutual humanity." Echoing the Martha mission of selfless compassion, she added, "Satisfaction starts with being able to give of our well-being to others," and this includes sharing skills and advice on food and nutrition, housekeeping, gardening, and financial and environmental issues that affect both individual families and the nation as a whole. "We must advance women's rights, gender equality, and women and girls' human rights," Marianne stressed in a recent conversation with me. When she needs inspiration and escape, Marianne has a simple solution—she heads into the woods. "The forest is an important soul landscape for me, a sacred oasis, a place of calm and rest," she explained.

At the Martha office in Joensuu, I asked Katja why their phones were ringing all the time. She answered, "Much of it is for our domestic work. Today, we received a call from a woman who is 103, and lives all by herself. She needs a cleaning service."

In years past, the Marthas developed such a strong reputation as domestic superwomen that a few Finns were intimidated by them. The perception, perhaps grounded in a bit of truth, was that they were an elite force of women who could do it all—knit socks, grow vegetables, raise hens, sell eggs, forage for food, juice and cook from scratch—all while raising children and having full-time jobs.

This skeptical attitude even extended, for a time, to a woman I met at the Martha office named Marja, whose great-aunt Augusta Laine was instrumental in the empowerment of women as a member of the Finnish Parliament, a founder of the Marthas of North Karelia in 1907, and its leader for forty years. She also founded Finland's first home economics school in 1919, which is now part of a national network of vocational schools that trains students to be profession-alized waiters, bakers, chefs, and hotel and other service workers. These vocational schools are secrets of Finland's impeccable customer and professional services in every sector of commerce. This consciousness starts early—home economics classes are provided in primary schools, where students learn how to cook and serve food they prepare in school test kitchens.

"It seemed like the Marthas could do anything, and knew everything," said Marja. "All the women in my family were Marthas while I was growing up. I didn't want to become a Martha. I didn't want to become one of those women who could knit and walk at the same time!" Amazed, I asked, "How do they do that?" Marja told me, "I looked closely at a Martha and saw that she had a pocket tied around her waist to carry a ball of yarn!" The women even held a competition to see who could walk more and knit the most. Marja continued, "I wanted to be who I am, not part of some association. But later, I realized that they were remarkable people who did remark-able work, and I joined them." Now she is one of the most active volunteers, and she notes proudly, "My great-grand-mother, grandmother, grand-aunt, mother, and my daughter and I have all been Marthas."

These Marthas were an incredibly impressive group of women, and I learned they had an intimate connection with the forest, as so many Finnish people have.

"One of our most enjoyable activities is to find edibles in the woods," added Ringa.

"Excuse me?" I asked.

"We teach people how to safely forage in the forest. The forest is our supermarket, our sanctuary, and our spiritual home. She always provides for us."

Ringa explained that Finland is a nation of people who love to go into the forest, off the main paths, and forage, or hand-harvest, the multitudes of berries and mushrooms that grow there. For Finns, Ringa noted, the forest is an abundant source of food. Finnish law and custom guarantees *Jokamiehen Oikeudet* (Everyman's Rights) to fish, swim, camp, have a picnic, and pick berries and mushrooms from pretty much everywhere in the nation, including private property, as long as nothing else is disturbed. Berries, mushrooms, and herbs are picked all over Finland, and the lush forests of Karelia are one of the richest sources. May, June, and July are prime times for harvesting roots and herbs, and summer and autumn are mushroom and berry season.

For weeks at a time from spring through fall, I learned, the forests of Finland are blanketed with scrumptious and sometimes poisonous mushrooms, and with juicy and nutritious wild berries. And for as long as anyone could remember, generations of Finns have been disappearing into the forest to gather natural delicacies like mushrooms, lingonberries, cloudberries, arctic brambleberries and bilberries (miniature cousins of the blueberry), nettle leaves, and birch sap, which is believed to have strong healing power. There are so many mushrooms and so few people in Finland less than 10 percent of all mushrooms in the country are picked.

The Finns bring their wild-picked mushrooms and berries home and turn them into traditional pies, rich sauces, soups, casseroles, hearty stews, and potent currant jams and juices to enjoy at summer cottages and through the long winter months. A summer treat from the lakes is crayfish, considered a national treasure. Some families have identified prime berry- and mushroom-foraging spots deep in the forest interior that are so prized that they keep the locations secret and pass the secret down through the generations, never revealing them to anyone outside the family or their small community.

This sounded intriguing. I already loved mushrooms, as certain types were a feature of the Japanese cuisine I grew up with. Shiitake mushrooms, for example, are a base of the vegetarian or vegan version of Japanese cooking broth. I even learned that mushrooms may have the power to reduce pollution and convert agricultural and industrial waste into foods and feed. I was eager to get up close and learn about them in their natural habitat of the Finnish forest.

I asked, "I want to go mushroom foraging with one of you. Could anyone take me along?" Ringa smiled and said, "Yes, there are Mushroom Marthas who can take you into the forest."

In the days and weeks that followed, I kept coming back to Martha headquarters, and I signed up for their foraging field trips, cooking classes, and mushroom lectures.

Soon I was tagging along with my new long-lost sisters all over Karelia.

The Nearly Total Silence

He wished that the whole Valley had been empty with plenty of room for dreams, you need space and silence to be able to fashion things sufficiently carefully.

—TOFT, IN TOVE JANSSON'S
MOOMINVALLEY IN NOVEMBER

A FEW DAYS LATER, WHILE walking through the forest along the Joensuu riverfront, I suddenly realized that it was indescribably quiet.

It was a truly startling feeling for someone used to a lifetime of noise in Tokyo and New York City. There was a powerful hush. I stopped to listen. I stopped, so my sneakers wouldn't make pebble-scraping noises on the narrow path that would cancel the silence.

The quiet stillness enveloped me. The world around me seemed to stand still. After a while of listening, I realized that I heard none of the noises that I was so accustomed to hearing in Manhattan, the cacophony of city life: cars honking, fire engine and ambulance sirens blaring, buses and trucks' roaring engines, people talking over others at restaurants, subway cars rattling and squeaking, and music blaring out of speakers in shops and cafés.

Ever since arriving in North Karelia, I had been constantly, consciously and unconsciously, comparing my surroundings in Joensuu with those in Manhattan and sometimes those in Tokyo, as almost anyone would do traveling to a new place. I then realized that not all differences are visible. One particularly striking difference in this new place was a peaceful quietness that is the absence of anthropogenic, or human-generated, sounds. Once I noticed this quietness as a pleasing character of my new environment, I noticed it even more. Everyday, everywhere I went, I was stunned with the serenity this quietness brought to me.

Sometimes, I could hear the sound of nearly total silence. I could hear sounds I never heard. No, not that I never heard, but the sounds I never noticed, and never really paid attention to. Like the sound of my own breathing. Like the whispers of the rustling wind and flowing streams, of leaves and tree branches brushing against each other, of the keening and chatter of distant birds, and the late summer air flowing around me. The faint awareness of the nearby Pielisjoki River rippling downstream to Lake Pyhäselkä. The earth was murmuring all around me.

Before I got here, I'd seen many beautiful landscapes of Finland on the internet and in travel books, and I had looked forward to experiencing this visually pleasing nation for myself. But I didn't anticipate the powerful effects of the nature sounds that accompanied these landscapes would have on my psyche, as well as the power of silences and the lack of urban noises.

The quietness I felt was not the complete absence of sounds. It was the lack of man-made noises I was so used to having all my life, having grown up and lived in big cities. It was the faint sounds of the earth's gentle murmurs, and nature's softly singing melodies. They were profoundly calming. "To listen to silence wherever you are, is an easy and direct way of becoming present," wrote the spiritual leader Eckhart Tolle. "Listening to the silence immediately creates stillness inside you."

When I asked Finnish women about their powerful love for the forest, they often described sensual and spiritual connections. The forest, they explained, is their supermarket, health club, spiritual retreat, and cathedral.

The earth was softly speaking to me. I heard no particular words. The rustling of nature was more like soothing music. They were subtle, welcoming embraces that tugged me gently and beckoned me to come home, to return to the forest.

I started to walk again with nature escorting me along the river. I heard more whispers and then I didn't hear anything. I walked toward the mouth of the river immersed in the surroundings aurally, visually, wholeheartedly.

I walked along in a serene trance.

The Forest Bath

The inhabitants are strong and hardy, with bright, intelligent faces, high cheek-bones, yellow hair in early life, and with brown hair in mature age. With regard to their social habits, morals, and manners, all travellers are unanimous in speaking well of them. Their temper is universally mild; they are slow to anger, and when angry they keep silence. They are happy-hearted, affectionate to one another, and honorable and honest in their dealings with strangers.

—JOHN MARTIN CRAWFORD
PREFACE TO THE FIRST ENGLISH
TRANSLATION OF THE *KALEVALA*, 1888

ONE DAY, PROFESSOR HELMI, WHO welcomed us on our first day in Finland, took us for a hike in the forest.

We began at her comfortable wooden house deep in the woods, where she lived with her husband, Matti Mäkelä, a brilliant, renowned Finnish writer and intellectual who was completing his doctoral degree in philosophy.

The house was perched in verdant splendor among towering spruce trees on the side of a hill that sloped toward an old-fashioned, wooden Finnish sauna hut, a rowboat, and a stream where Matti caught perch for us to enjoy for brunch that morning.

On the walk and afterward, Helmi told us of the powerful hold the forest had on her life, and her memories. She grew up on a small farm in western Finland, with a backyard that consisted of a forest that went on for twenty-five miles before it reached another house. In summer, the forest was filled with lingonberries and bilberries, she and her siblings made improvised toys from things in the forest, and spent much of their childhood outdoors. Bilberries are a European native berry related to North American blueberries, but they are smaller and darker blue than American blueberries.

"We were always in the forest," she recalled, "and I loved it." The sounds, sights, and smells are vivid in her memory many years later. "One day when I was four or five years old I was lying down in the middle of a little forest of Arctic star flowers. I remember crawling around, then lying there and feeling, *I am a part of this.* Somebody once said that I carry the calmness of the forest with me."

"I have a very strong sense memory from being a child in the forest," Helmi told me. "I can remember smells and sounds from all the seasons. Autumn was my favorite season;

it brought the rich smell of rotting mushrooms. In the winter was the snow and frost, in the spring was the beautiful sharp smell of birches coming out, then there was the bright smell of hay in summer and the sound of my favorite bird, the Kuovi, or Eurasian curlew."

She continued, "If I'm not able to go to the forest for some time, I'm not happy. It's a kind of yearning that comes inside me. I am only completed when I'm in the forest. You can be free in the forest and you can breathe fresh air. I am of the opinion that trees, especially pines, have a lot of energy inside of them. In Finland, if a father and son were working in the forest and the son got tired, the father would say go and put your back against a pine, and that will give you energy. It was truly believed you could get energy from a tree! So if I am very tired I will go and hug a pine tree."

"I can confess," Helmi concluded, "that I am a tree hugger."

When she said this, I thought, *I'm a tree hugger, too! Maybe this is a universal human need, to be in the forest and bask in the beauty and power of trees—I need more of this in my life.*

I remembered back to when I was in my early twenties, working a high-pressure junior job at an American advertising agency based in Tokyo's Otemachi district. After graduating from university in Illinois, I had returned to Tokyo for my first job, worked crazy hours, and commuted to work on sardine-packed trains. I was part of a generation whose parents and grandparents had rebuilt postwar Japan into the economic miracle of "Japan Inc." and the world's second biggest economy. Unfortunately, the social norm was still to work brutal hours of overtime, skip vacation days, and sacrifice your personal time to serve your company, factory, or office. I missed the wide-open spaces of the United States. I craved tranquility, and time and space for myself.

On many weekends, I escaped the super-populated city and hiked in forested hills and sculpted gardens of Buddhist temples in Kamakura, the site of the Kamakura Shogunate from 1185 to 1333, about an hour and a half south of Tokyo by express train. I missed my friends from my college years in the United States, and I suffered from massive reverse-culture shock when I went back to Japan. I fled to the peace and serenity of Kamakura as kind of a survival mode, and participated in Zen meditation sessions there for the first time in my life. I was desperate for some space and quiet to center and ground myself. The trees in Japan gave me energy, just as they did for Helmi in Finland. But since I didn't have a very clear awareness of what I was doing and its positive effect, and I was a creature of my environment, unfortunately for me I gradually assimilated back to the urban workaholic lifestyle.

Then the ad agency I worked for in Tokyo agreed to transfer me to its headquarters in the United States. I flew from Tokyo to Manhattan, where skyscrapers symbolized success, our offices were called sweatshops, and I rarely saw soil or sky beyond the glories of Central Park, which was con-sidered often too crime-ridden and dangerous to venture into at the time. New York City had the added issue of huge levels of street, subway, and traffic noise, which can do real damage to your health over time. "Chronic noise contributes to stress, annoyance, cardiovascular problems, sleep disturbance, and decreased task performance," reported a team of researchers in a paper published in the *International Journal of Environmental Research and Public Health* in 2017. "It has both psychological and physical effects ranging from elevated blood pressure, poor sustained attention, and memory problems to sleep disturbances, increased risk of myocardial infarction, annoyance, and learned helplessness. These effects can occur below our level of awareness."

It would take many years, and a voyage to Finland, for me to fully realize how much we need nature, perhaps because we *are* nature. Finland, I discovered, is one of the world capitals of trees, lakes, and peace and quiet, even in cities.

An intriguing window into the world of trees has opened up in recent years with the pioneering work of forest ecology professor Suzanne Simard and her colleagues at the University of British Columbia. Through their experiments, they've discovered that trees are connected with each other through underground mycorrhizal networks, or fungal threads, that link up with tree roots to comprise a vast "wood-wide web" of organic circuitry that enables trees to cooperate, exchange nutrients and water, and even share information and send distress signals. The networks are hidden underground, and operate on an infinitesimally slower time scale than human speed, but they are humming away all the time, all around the planet.

This scientific view of a forest as having a central nervous system is reflected in stories of cooperating, communicating, and sentient trees that appear in Greek, Norse, Mesoamerican, Irish, and Japanese folklore. "Everything is connected, absolutely everything," noted Sm'hayetsk Teresa Ryan, a Canadian forest ecologist of Indigenous Tsimshian heritage who has studied mycorrhizal networks with Simard. "There are many aboriginal groups that will tell you stories about how all the species in the forests are connected, and many will talk about below-ground networks."

In the Finnish folklore epic the *Kalevala*, trees enter into dialogues with people, provide protection to them, and feel sorrow when attacked by people. And if forests are, in a scientific sense, superorganisms of individual trees linked together by fungal networks, then Finland's sprawling woodlands of spruce, pine, and birch are shining examples of the triumph of a species.

Back in 1982, my heavily forested home country of Japan was the birthplace of *shinrin-yoku* (forest bathing), a phrase that was coined by Tomohide Akiyama, who was then the secretary of the Japanese Forestry Agency. He thought of the phrase as a way of promoting physical and mental health through nature-based health and wellness activities like *kaisui-yoku* (ocean bathing), *nikko-yoku* (sun bathing) and *onsen-yoku* (hot spring bathing). Forest bathing didn't refer to taking a bath in forest, but to the act of walking, relaxing, and breathing in the woods and savoring the sounds, smells, and feelings of nature. When a person travels through a forest, the theory goes, they enjoy a "five senses experience," of sight, smell, hearing, touch, and taste. The concept's tagline used by the Japanese Forestry Agency was "bathe in the forest atmosphere, and fortify mind and body."

It turns out that forest bathing, forest walking, forest immersion, and similar nature-based activities offer a wide range of mental and physical health benefits that have been reported in research published in peer-reviewed scientific and medical journals.

In two major research papers published in 2019, teams of European and Chinese experts reported that forest bathing may significantly improve people's mental and physical health by providing multiple benefits that reinforce each other. Their research indicates that forest bathing can regulate blood pressure and pulse rate, regulate endocrine activity, reduce blood glucose, relieve depression, foster a sense of calm and security, decrease negative emotions and anxiety, reduce levels of the stress biomarker cortisol, promote a healthier immune system, improve mood and attention, assist in recovery from mental fatigue, improve cardiac-pulmonary parameters, and enhance psychological stress recovery and well-being.

Some of the most striking research on forest bathing has been spearheaded by Dr. Qing Li, MD, PhD, a physician and immunologist at Nippon Medical School Hospital in Tokyo, who is considered the world's foremost expert in the new field of "forest medicine." Dr. Li and his colleagues have found through experiments that periods of forest bathing significantly enhance both intracellular anticancer proteins and NK (natural killer) cells, which help the body fight viruses and tumor formation. The effect lasts for seven days or more after the forest bath. "One of the mechanisms that facilitate these therapeutic benefits comes directly from the forest air itself," reported Marianna Pogosyan, a lecturer in cultural psychology. "Phytoncides are volatile organic compounds that are exuded from trees and plants and act as protective agents

against harmful insects. Inhaling these natural forest fra-
grances drives some of the positive effects of the forest on our
physiological functioning."

The nation of Finland is one giant forest bath, as it is the
European nation with the highest percentage of its surface
area covered by forest, about 72 percent, and a great many
Finnish people live, play, walk, and exercise inside, or in very
close proximity to, forests and other green spaces. This might
help explain the Finnish people's world-topping performance
in so many global rankings, including happiness and health.

Forest bathing may be one of the great health and happiness secrets of Finland, and there is another national practice
that may be just as powerful.

The Vapor Bath

They are a cleanly people, being much given to the use of vapor-baths. This trait is a conspicuous note of their character from their earliest history to the present day. Often in the runes of The Kalevala reference is made to the "cleansing and healing virtues of the vapors of the heated bathroom."

—JOHN MARTIN CRAWFORD
PREFACE TO THE FIRST ENGLISH
TRANSLATION OF THE *KALEVALA*, 1888

ONE DAY, WILLIAM MET A fellow dad in Joensuu who was doing acrobatics with his six-year old daughter on a sports field.

The dad, a young sports trainer named Juhamatti, became fast friends with William, and later that year when the weather got cold and icy he invited our family to the *Joensuun Jääkarhut* (winter swimming center) otherwise known as the Joensuu Polar Bears ice swimming club. There, Juhamatti introduced us to the classic Finnish tradition of sitting in a piping hot sauna, running down to a hole in the ice on a lake, immersing yourself in freezing cold water, running back to the sauna, then repeating the cycle several times.

We had been enjoying the little electric-powered sauna room that was built into our rental apartment in Joensuu, but this was a whole different concept. The sensation of repeatedly, rapidly immersing yourself alternately in ice water and a heated sauna is a shocking and invigorating enough experience, but the sauna at the Joensuu Polar Bears center was a large communal, unisex sauna.

We were sitting facing several strangers a few feet in front of us, mostly silent Finnish men, women, and children, all of us in swimsuits and sweating our faces off in 180 degree Fahrenheit thick steam. Now and then someone would pour scoops of water on the hot stones to fire up the heat, then gently smack themselves on the chest and back with a *vihta*, or *vasta* (sauna whisk made of birch branches) to stimulate the warm skin. The Finnish sauna experience reminded me of the communal hot springs rituals I grew up with in Japan, where families and friends take trips to a mountainside *ryokan* (a type of traditional Japanese inn) to soak and relax in a giant hot spring, often outdoors. Afterward, we would dress in *yukata* (casual kimono robes) and enjoy a hearty dinner sitting on Japanese thin cushions on tatami-mat floors. It is a relaxing, cleansing, rejuvenating social activity, like the Finnish sauna.

Finland is the sauna capital of the world—the small nation that accounts for fully half the planet's sauna sales. There is, on average, one sauna for every family in the nation.

Until the 1960s, many Finnish babies were born in saunas since they were considered very safe places of health and hygiene, and today, many Finnish children are gently introduced to the sauna lifestyle at as young as four or five months of age. A Finnish saying to children is *"saunassa pitaa olla kuin kirkossa,"* or "in the sauna you must behave as if you were in a church." Misbehavior is forbidden in the sauna, otherwise the sauna elf, or *saunatonttu,* will burn it down. For adults, this usually means no food in the sauna, and no discussing controversial subjects.

A majority of the Finnish population visits a sauna at least once a week, and it is often the scene of business, social, and family get-togethers. For me, the effect of sitting in a sauna is almost like meditation. It gives me peace, relaxation, contemplation, and contentment in the moment, and a wonderfully mellow post-sauna buzz that lasts for an hour or more afterward. I could see why the Finns loved it so much. Also, the sauna is a social equalizer. In the sauna, everyone is equal, whether naked or wrapped in a towel, since there are no clothes or jewelry to distract from talking with your friends or just zoning out with perfect strangers.

"What makes a sauna a venue for social events is not just the common experience inside the sauna but the gathering afterwards," wrote the Finland-based author Harald Haarmann. "Family members and friends sit together, share a meal and enjoy themselves." As the Vancouver-based, Finnish-born designer Petra Kaksonen wrote, "There are few more quintessentially Finnish summer traditions than skinny-dipping in a lake at midnight after spending hours in a sauna, roasting *makkara* (sausage) on an open fire and sitting in semi-silence contemplating the meaning of life (there is no need for unnecessary small talk in Finland) while fighting against an army of mosquitoes."

The sauna can be used as a relaxed, intimate setting for discussing delicate political or business affairs, and a place to contemplate big decisions on your own. Finland's longtime head of state Urho Kekkonen, who was the president for a full twenty-six years until 1982 explained, "In the sauna I relax physically and invigorate mentally. The calm atmosphere creates harmony. For me, life without a sauna would be completely impossible." The same is true of many Finnish people. When building a new house in Finland, it was a traditional practice for a family to live in the sauna hut first, while the main house was being built.

A Finnish friend named Sanna told me of the all-important marriage ritual of the prewedding bachelorette party, or "bridal sauna." The bride-to-be and her bridesmaids, she explained, go into the sauna together and discuss marriage and relationship advice, and even love spells. The sweating bride wears a T-shirt belonging to her future husband, is smacked on the back with birch branches by her girlfriends to make the point that married life isn't problem-free, and to emphasize recommendations like "always kiss each other goodnight" and "let him feel like he's in charge even though you are in control." The bride runs around the sauna and calls out all the names of her former boyfriends to expunge their spirits, and after the sauna she is given an egg shampoo to symbolize fertility.

Juhamatti, our host at the Joensuu sauna, told us, "This is one of the best things you can do for your health." He had a point. The old Finnish proverb *"sauna on köyhän apteekki"*—"the sauna is the poor man's apothecary"—has a basis in science. Recent research has suggested that sauna bathing is associated with reduced cardiovascular mortality and reduction in the risks of high blood pressure, stroke, neurocognitive diseases, pulmonary diseases, dementia, and all-cause mortality.

The quintessential Finnish sauna is a small wooden hut that stands close to the edge of a lake, a river, or a bay, a few yards away from a cabin or a cottage. In apartment buildings, there can be a communal sauna, or if you're really lucky, an individual sauna room is included in your apartment, powered not by fire but by an efficient electrical heater.

In the sauna, one finds a changing area, a shower area, and a sauna room with sitting benches, usually upper and lower levels along the interior walls, and a heating mechanism like a wood-burning stove, or *kiuas*, and heated stones, or *kiuaskivet*, upon which ladles full of water are poured, creating steam, or *löyly*. If you're sitting closest to the water bucket, or *kiulu*, you're in charge of throwing water on the hot rocks. Same-sex and family saunas are usually in the nude, but it's okay to wear a towel or swimwear at a public sauna.

The room temperature usually ranges from 150 to 195 degrees Fahrenheit, and the typical routine is to sit in the sauna for fifteen to twenty minutes, work up a good sweat, take a cool rinse in a shower or body of water, then repeat, for a total experience of around ninety minutes. According to Kalevi Ruuska, the Finnish-born cofounder of the North American Sauna Society, "The heat from the sauna and a sudden cooling gives you an extreme rush of hormones like endorphin. Afterwards you feel light and happy. The bigger the change in the temperature, the stronger the effect is too." He adds, "Any Finn would argue that enjoying the blissful body and soul-warming heat in the privacy of your home sauna is an essential and much needed part of everyday life."

KATJA'S FRIEND SANNA appeared with a basket full of evergreen branches and set them before us, saying her father had picked them for us in the morning.

Katja and I were relaxing in cool summer breezes overlooking Lake Koitere, and pink geranium and orange nasturtium blossoms adorned the dark brown log-cabin terrace.

Sanna returned with a bucket and a kettle of hot water. She transferred the branches to the bucket, and poured the hot water. This was the beginning of a do-it-yourself, informal "aromatherapy spa" hosted by Sanna at her family cottage. She worked at the Karelia University of Applied Science in Joensuu, and later became an entrepreneur running a gluten-free bakery with her sister.

We plucked a few big clusters of purple-pink rosebay willowherb (*Chamaenerion angustifolium*) flowers from the backyard, and placed them in buckets full of hot water. We transferred them into the sauna room, where Sanna had already submerged *vihta*, or *vasta* (bundles of birch branches) in another bucket of water.

The sauna was built with rustic dark brown/black logs and a tiny window with a view of the garden and lake, the bottom half of it covered with a white lace curtain with traditional Karelian bird and flower patterns. High and low benches were affixed against the back wall. We sat on the high bench with our feet soaking in the hot rosebay willowherb water. I felt the tensions being unlocked and released from my toes and feet, and gradually from the rest of my body.

Sanna shook the birch branches over a heap of hot stones in the corner of the sauna room. The room was instantly filled with hot steam. She handed a branch to each of us, and we slapped them on our backs, arms, and legs with giddy laughter.

Katja reached for a ladle and scooped water from a wooden sauna bucket, both of which were fixtures of every sauna, and threw the water onto the hot stones. They hissed, filling the room with more steam, making the air piping hot. The heat felt so good to my skin, mind, and soul. The sensation reminded me of a Japanese *onsen*. The heat made me breathe deeply a few times. I smelled the birch, pines, rosebay flowers, wood of the sauna room in the moist air. When the steam cleared, and the temperature was declining, I threw a ladle full of water to the hot stones to keep the heat going.

Once our pores were open, I applied black peat mud to my face and all over my body, following my friends' examples. This was the highlight of Sanna's "spa treatment." I was fascinated with this natural facial and body wrap gathered from a nearby marsh. Peat is described by *Encyclopedia Britannica* as "fuel consisting of spongy material formed by the partial decomposition of organic matter, primarily plant material, in wetlands such as swamps, muskegs, bogs, fens, and moors." As a fuel source, burnt peat is considered environmentally unfriendly, but as a spa treatment it is highly refreshing and rejuvenating, and credited by researchers to possess antiallergic, antibacterial, anti-inflammatory, and antiviral effects.

We sat in silence covered with the black mud, drenched in the hot air, feeling any stress and tension slowly released from our bodies and minds. Time stood still. It was a meditative cleansing ritual. Once in a while one of us threw water over the stones to keep the heat going. Steam billowed and filled the room. Once we were super hot we walked over and slid into the lake, and the cool water delivered an invigorating sensation.

I submerged my head under the water. Just like when I walked in a thick forest, I was once again one with Mother Earth. We swam and floated in twilight. The water surface was calm and flat. There was no one else but us in the lake as far as I could see. Blue-pink light illuminated the western sky.

Our supper was Omega 3–rich salmon salad with leafy greens and herbs from the garden, home-baked quiche served with white currant wine, and fresh berries for dessert on the porch. Our faces were glowing in the pink-orange twilight, now covering much of the late summer evening.

Everything we were enjoying came from the pure nature surrounding the cottage—the backyard, lake, river, woods, and nearby swamp.

I wondered, *What do they buy from the supermarket?* I thought for a while, and all I could think of was toilet paper.

Visions of Karelia

When the days and nights were brighter,
When the fir-trees shone like sunlight,
And the birches like the moonbeams;
Honey breathed throughout the forest,
Settled in the glens and highlands
Spices in the meadow-borders,
Oil out-pouring from the lowlands.

—THE *KALEVALA*

AS THE LATE SUMMER BLENDED into fall, Katja and her friend Jenny, a national Martha leader and Helsinki-born business consultant-turned-dairy-farmer in the Finnish border town of Ilomantsi, took me further and deeper into Karelia.

We hiked in hushed woods and hills; foraged for mushrooms, berries, and herbs; and savored the company of local Marthas we encountered in each town and village.

Our itineraries unfolded in a stream of exotically Tolk-
ienesque place-names, as my guides told me: "Early in the
morning we will drive to Kesälahti, where I'll take you into
the first forest. We will have lunch in Kesälahti, perhaps in the
garden of Sovintola. After lunch we will go to another forest,
in Ruokkee. Then we will drive via a beautiful ridge way to the
Hotelli Punkaharju to have dinner. From Punkaharju it's not
a long way to the town of Savonlinna. Then we will take you
home to Joensuu via Kerimäki, Villala, Puhos—on the way,
there is world's biggest wooden church, so perhaps we will
stop by there."

On these drives, with each bend in the road, I became more
appreciative of the gentle elevations and hills that often surfaced
on a new horizon. There were no mountain peaks or fjords here,
but somehow the excitement of seeing the looming small hills
that unfolded here and there could be just as thrilling.

The writer Leslie Li described the landscapes of a nearby
district in these romantic terms: "Kuopio almost dissolves
into a tapestry of densely packed evergreen forests, pale-green
fields of rye set off by an occasional red-ocher farmhouse and
deep-blue Kallavesi Lake below, with darker lakes far beyond,
all of them studded with scores of emerald-green islands even
more primeval than their surroundings." According to the
Australian journalist Matt Bolton, "Finland may not have the
geographical splendor of her cousins Norway and Iceland, but
the endless forests and lakes which take on a hypnotic hall-of-
mirrors effect as they repeat eternally into the distance gen-
erate a passion so palpable, it is hard to resist." I knew exactly
what he meant.

The Mushroom Queen

Then the trees began to grow,
All the slender saplings stretching;
Pine trees spread their bushy tops
And the spruces flower-crowned.
Birches lifted from the hollows,
From the light loam alders rose;
In the bogs the chokecherry bloomed
Beaded with abundant fruit;
On the barrens junipers,
Beautiful with berry clusters.

—The *Kalevala*

"GO ON, PICK IT," SAID Päivi the Mushroom Queen.

"I'm afraid," I mumbled.

She pointed to a prominent-looking mushroom standing exposed all by itself on the pine needle– and twig-laden ground. It had a saucer-like brown cap two inches in diameter and a sturdy beige stem.

The mushroom looked so picture perfect that I thought I might accidentally mutilate it while trying to separate it from Mother Earth.

I was wandering in a dense forest with master mushroom forager Päivi and a group of several other Marthas. My boots squished on an uneven, cushiony carpet of moss and fallen leaves, giving my knees, legs, and back a tender workout.

An hour earlier, before we set off on our hike, Päivi opened her car trunk in the parking lot and produced a supply of homemade mushroom cookies and a Thermos full of delightfully mellow, nutty-vanilla-tasting chaga mushroom tea to enjoy. Chaga mushrooms (*Inonotus obliquus*) appear as charcoal-black clusters on the side of birch trees, with a golden brown interior, and for centuries they've been used in traditional medicine in Finland, Russia, and elsewhere. Today, chaga can be enjoyed as a tea or as a powder or liquid to add to soups or smoothies, and researchers are finding that there may indeed be health benefits from the mushroom, including antioxidant, anticancer, antiviral, anti-inflammatory and pro-immune system effects.

Fortified by tea-and-cookie mushroom power, we set off into the woods. There was no path and no trace of civilization, only birch, pine, and spruce trees rolling over gentle hills in all directions. My eyes scanned around a magical landscape of lush, expansive vegetation, layers of bright green moss- and whitish-gray reindeer lichen–covered rocks, one-foot-tall miniature trees, fallen branches, twigs and leaves, ferns, low berry bushes, wild flowers and grasses, an ant hill, white birch trunks, stately dark brown pine trunks soaring into the sky, and some fallen trunks leaning on top of each other. Glittering light streamed through leaves, branches, and tree trunks, casting diagonal streaks and shadows in the forest.

I inhaled rich vapors of moist pine, heard hushed conversations of wispy wind and birch leaves, and sensed my breathing synchronized with natures' pulses. My physical, emotional, and spiritual beings were completely blending with the surroundings. The most profound sensation of bliss filled my body and soul, a mystical sensation that I had never known existed or was possible.

After spending some time in the forests of Karelia, I came to realize that fairy tales I had read when I was a child were not quite fairy tales, but somehow real. As one visitor from Sydney, Australia, a woman named Ali Noble, explained, "Stepping into a Finnish forest is something akin to being in a childhood fairytale: lush, soft lichen underfoot; big red toadstools; tall green trees; and the suspicion that if a fairy did appear, you wouldn't be too surprised." If I came across a group of fairies in this thick enchanted forest, I certainly would not have been surprised at all. I would have understood. Even if I could not see them, they were there, watching over us.

You never forget spotting your first mushroom in a Finnish forest. At least I never will. Sometimes they appear in great congregations on a sloping hillside; other times they poke up flamboyantly as psychedelic-colored exhibitionists from the base of a tree; or as solitary, stately monuments, like this one.

I kneeled down to examine the mushroom spotted by Päivi the Mushroom Queen. This was a trophy mushroom, a porcini (*Boletus edulis*), a type especially cherished in Italy for its aroma, dense texture, and earthy-rich flavor. Like most mushrooms, this was an engineering marvel, conferring great dignity to the word *fungus*, which describes all mushrooms. It was barely three inches tall, and it was magnificent. The porcini stood there as if to say, "I am here!" I could only stare at its beauty and stature.

It had such a gorgeous shape and regal, commanding presence—a perfect sculpture by Mother Nature—that I was afraid to touch the mushroom, let alone remove it from the earth.

Päivi kindly said, "I will show you."

With her guidance, I pushed my fingers into the ground, reaching the bottom of the stem, and gently pulled it out. I shaved the soiled area around the bottom with a brush-tipped mushroom knife, being mindful not to take any more flesh than I needed to. I sliced it vertically in halves and examined the specimen. Clean, white interiors. No worms or bite marks. What a beauty! I placed the halves in the basket like laying down a newborn baby in a bassinet.

We walked deeper into the forest toward a hill. There was no path, just random zigzag patches of clearer ground amid the rocks and fallen branches. Päivi pointed to a mushroom a few feet away. I marveled at how she could see it camouflaged in the environment. Different mushrooms, she explained, prefer the company of different trees: orange- and yellow-colored chanterelles (*Cantharellus*), for example, like birch forests, while *Boletus* mushrooms like spruce and pine forests. She approached and picked the small reddish-brown mushroom, which had a one-inch-diameter cap.

She neatly sliced off the bottom of the soil-covered stem with a mushroom knife, dropped the tip, and brushed off dirt and plant specks from the cap with the brush attached to the other end of the knife handle. She closely examined the mushroom and announced, "This is a curry milk cap (*Lactarius camphoratus*)." She slit the gills. White liquid dotted the incision.

"See, milk," Päivi said. I knew about this treasured mushroom. Another Finnish friend, Anu, a food writer and stylist, recipe developer and chef in Helsinki, had told me how a tiny amount of dried little bits of this mushroom could add an amazing curry aroma to a dish.

Päivi placed the mushroom in her basket. I noticed more on the ground. I picked up one and asked, "Is this a curry milk cap too?" Päivi said, "Yes." Hooray! Now I could guess a small percentage of what I found! The number one golden rule of foragers is pick and eat only what you can identify 100 percent for sure, or you may be poisoned. Which is why I didn't plan on foraging alone.

Päivi stopped and picked up a medium-sized green-grayish mushroom with corrugated edges around the cap.

"This is good," she said. "This is a *hapero* (russula, *Russula*)." She cleaned it and put it into the basket. I thought to myself, *I never would have guessed that this would be a good mushroom, because the colors looked moldy. Sorry, hapero!*

Päivi moved briskly through the forest focusing on spotting "good" mushrooms. I picked two promising mushrooms, caught up with her, and asked, "How about these?" She glanced and quickly said, "No. Not good." I tossed them to the ground. Päivi added, "They're not poisonous. But they're not good. We don't eat it."

She picked another mushroom, "This is a milk cap." I asked, "A regular one?" "Yes." She cleaned it and put it into a small paper bag in the basket. She was separating them from others, as she'd first boil them in water for ten minutes to rid them of their tartness.

I found more curry milk caps hidden under ferns and leaves around mossy rocks. I showed them to Päivi and she nodded. I cleaned them and placed them in the basket. I felt proud that I was getting good at it, though I still needed an expert to verify. I picked a mushroom and asked, "Is this a milk cap?" Päivi, "Yes, but it's not a good one." She added, "It's so small." I repeated, "It's small . . . ok," I tossed it, puzzled.

For some mushrooms, like chanterelles, small was good because they were packed with flavor. I picked two mushrooms and asked, "These are no good, right?" Päivi perked up. "Not this one, but this one is very good!" pointing to a very dark brown mushroom. "It's a *nokirousku* (chocolate milk mushroom, *Lactarius lignyotus*)!" she said excitedly. A small, three-quarter-inch diameter, very dark-brown cap with white gills and a long, skinny dark-brown stem. I saw more of the same. I picked them, and asked, "Are they good?" "Yes," she said. "This one, too?" I asked. Päivi said, "Yes. Yes, these are very good. They're milk caps but they can go directly into a pan." There was no need to boil them like regular milk caps. I mumbled to myself, "You never know which ones are good."

She took a few steps, bent down and picked another. "This is also a hapero." She sliced off the bottom of its stem, and looking at the cut section of the stem, said, "A very good one. See, no worms." She sliced the stem and the cap vertically in exact halves. Yes, I saw that it was a clean, beautiful mushroom. "You're going to eat this," she said, smiling.

Päivi said, "This one is a *haaparousku* (northern milk cap, *Lactarius trivialis*)," holding up a grayish-purple cap mushroom about two inches in diameter. It was quite exotic and beautiful. She added, "You need to cook this one for five minutes to reduce its tartness."

Päivi picked a reddish cap mushroom, cleaned the stem, peeled the thin red skin, cut a small piece of white flesh, and handed it to me. She sliced another piece and put it into her mouth. I put mine into my mouth, tasted it, and immediately spat it out. "It's so peppery!" We both laughed.

We soon found small and medium-size chanterelles (*Cantharellus cibarius*), another prized treasure from the forest. Päivi disappeared into the woods and came out with creamy white mushrooms with warped caps. She said, "They are *vaaleaorakas* (wood hedgehog or hedgehog mushroom, *Hydnum repandum*)! I was looking for these!" happily announcing her feat.

With our baskets filled with treasures from the forest, we headed to Sovintola, a handicraft and culture center that included a full rustic kitchen that we could use. First, we sorted the foraged mushrooms on a large table on an outdoor terrace. Päivi took us through the characteristics of each variety.

She brought them into the kitchen and proceeded to slice and sauté several varieties of mushrooms with butter in a frying pan. "This is the best way," she told me as I looked over her shoulder. The aromas of heated butter and mushrooms filled the kitchen, my nostrils, and my month. The mushroom flesh was getting golden brown, and the edges crusty. She flipped each slice expertly with two forks making sure not to overcook. Then it was lunchtime.

First, we sampled the pan-sautéed mushrooms we picked only two hours ago. My heart pitter-pattering, I pierced a piece with a fork and brought it carefully into my mouth. I contemplated its flavors, textures, aromas, and all the nuances in between. I tasted the earth, raindrops, dried pine needles, mosses, and above all, Mother Nature's love. Everyone was quiet. We didn't have to say anything.

Päivi, the forager-chef, then served porcini-cream soup garnished with dried slices of porcini. Fantastic. Next, she served toasted rye bread topped with spruce-tip pesto, followed by blocks of bread cheese (or Finnish "squeaky cheese" in the United States) with yellowfoot (*Craterellus tubaeformis*) jam, which might sound strange but is totally delicious. For dessert, she brought out lingonberry-carrot Karelian pies and yellowfoot mushroom cookies, which were a perfect way to conclude our mushroom feast—all homemade, except the cheese.

While much of the world was relying on overprocessed, overindustrialized food, here in North Karelia, the Marthas were upholding the great Finnish tradition of a wilderness-to-table food lifestyle, nurtured by their everyday relationships with nature.

We stared at the rich gifts from nature with gratitude and pride.

It was the "wildest" meal of my life.

As a farewell gift, Päivi gave me a bottle of homemade chaga elixir, which she instructed me to take a small spoonful of daily.

Wild Herbs

ON A GORGEOUS LATE SUMMER morning, I joined a field trip to the Kolvananuuro Nature Reserve, a wilderness area twenty-two miles from Joensuu in the foothills of Eno in the municipality of Kontiolahti, a trip led by two Marthas named Maija and Kaarina. They were passionate about wild edibles and eager to pass on their knowledge. As soon as we arrived at the reserve, even before we left the parking lot, they began pointing out plants and offering detailed descriptions.

A few steps into the forest, Maija bent down to pull out a tiny cream-colored mushroom, barely 0.3 inches in diameter. She brushed off small dirt clumps to reveal one little pine needle attached to the bottom of the stringy mushroom stem. She explained, "Each pine needle produces one mushroom. That's why there are so many." I looked down on the ground and noticed for the first time many creamy, baby mushrooms dotting all over the carpet of fallen pine leaves.

The Kolvananuuro Gorge is a mini Grand Canyon, and a rare geographic feature for Finland, featuring sloping tree-covered cliffs that plunge down 250 feet to a winding stream. The gorge is a remnant of the chain of Alps–like Karelides Mountains that were here two billion years ago and mostly flattened by ice ages and erosion. When the ice melted, the water washed away sand from the gorge walls, creating a sand delta over nine thousand years ago. There's a variety of hiking trails here, so you can choose your route depending upon your desired ease/difficulty, length, and time frame. We chose a relatively easy flat trail to a designated public campfire site, 1.3 miles one-way. The trails were well-marked and family-friendly.

On our leisurely hike, we saw varying vegetation, from shady pockets of old-growth pines, spruces, junipers, birches, alders and aspens, to swampy fields and bogs, patches of rocky, barren terrain, and a pond adorned with water lilies.

After a few minutes of walking through an area graced by large fern plants, I heard the gurgling of a stream rushing down the grassy hill. Maija said, "You can drink this water." Kaarina bent down by the stream, scooped a palmful of water and brought it to her mouth. I did the same.

Soon we came upon wooden planks laid over swampy fields. Maija and Kaarina pointed to bright orange berries in the fields, exclaiming, "*Lakka* (Cloudberries, *Rubus chamaemorus*)!" They picked a sample of the prized, extra-nutritious berries and handed them to me. I popped them in my mouth. As I chewed the berries, their tart, sweet juices burst, and my teeth crunched seeds that are rich in Omega 6,

Omega 3, vitamin E, vitamin A, and plant sterols—all good for my health.

How beautiful these bright orange-gold berries looked dotting in the moist field. They weren't anything like the ones in plastic containers I saw at farmers' markets in town squares. I learned that bright-orange ones were not ripe yet. I learned that when the color became peachy orange evenly throughout a berry, and sepals protecting the berry faced downward, the berry was ripe.

When we came to the public campfire spot, our turning point, I asked the Marthas why they come to the forest. Kaarina answered, "To lower blood pressure. For feeling great. Fresh air. To be together with people I love. And to sit by an open fire." She smiled and pointed to a family with three dogs sitting around an open fire roasting sausages. She added, "I love that we are able to pick berries, and find other things in the forest we can eat."

I was feeling the same kind of pleasure and satisfaction as I went foraging in the wilderness with the Marthas. It was like discovering a primal survival skill I never knew I had, and was proud to practice using. It was a calming sensation, and also the realization of a fundamental truth that food comes from nature, not from stores.

Kaarina continued, "Mostly I go to forests to have a relaxing time." Maija added, "You feel all the senses: you see, smell, taste, hear everything more deeply and powerfully. If you're stressed, forests are the best place to come. It's very good for brains!" She continued, "Our history is in the forest. We have been in towns only for very short time." Maija said, "Our souls are in the forest. Particularly, my soul."

I asked, "Do you feel like this is home? Do you feel this is a place where you truly belong?"

Maija replied, "It's my church. Nature. Yes. This is our church."

At home that night, I rinsed a few leaves of stone bramble (*Rubus saxatilis*), a wild edible plant we picked in a field that day, and steeped them in a pot of hot water, as Majra and Kaarina taught me. In a quiet kitchen with a dimmed light, I sipped the fresh herb tea, so warm and calming.

Soon I was ready for a long, peaceful sleep.

Berry Joy

I STOOD ON THE EDGE of a small garden of rich, dark, soft soil.

I was in the village of Kinahmo, thirty-four miles north of Joensuu, visiting another Martha foraging expert named Päivi for a master class in forest berry picking. She was a faculty member at the University of Eastern Finland. Päivi grew vegetables and berries for her family in this garden. Several milking cows were grazing idyllically nearby.

My friend Katja disappeared behind a tall vegetable bush and came back out with a fistful of young tender peas for me to taste. Sweet, fresh flavors burst in my mouth while I chewed the soft-crunchy pods.

I walked around the garden and found a dense raspberry bush. I spotted ripe berries hanging on branches and gently pulled one between my fingers. Pop! Raspberry juice filled my mouth.

Päivi and her sister-in-law Raili, also a Martha, took Katja and me to a nearby forest to pick bilberries. We drove a few minutes in a country landscape, and Päivi swung the car onto a dirt road running through the forest. As soon as we got out of the car, Päivi and Raili started marching directly into the thick forest—no paths, trails, nor markers—as if in a trance, scooping berries from low bushes with a berry picker.

I followed them into the forest and looked around. Bilberries everywhere! I bent down, picked a couple of berries, and threw them into my mouth.

It was a heavenly taste—rich, tangy, and sugary.

I then started to pick more with a berry picker, a small container with a rake at the opening for easy berry picking and a handle for holding. Päivi came over and said, "Hold the bottom of the branches with your left hand like this, then scoop berries with the picker like this," gesturing the move. We briskly swept the area. Päivi marched away, scooping more berries.

I scooped berries, took a few steps, scooped berries, took a few more steps, and scooped some more. *I could do this all day*, I thought to myself.

I was becoming "one with the berries" and the act of picking them.

I followed the foraging rhythm my friend Anu taught me: "the first handful goes to your mouth, the next handful goes to your basket, the next your mouth, and the next to your basket."

I heard nothing except the bottoms of my waterproof pants rustling the low bushes and my hiking boots walking on a soft, cushiony ground covered with moss, ferns, fallen leaves, and branches. I enjoyed every sensation I felt all over my feet, legs, and back as I slowly walked on this most luxurious carpet that nature had rolled out for me. I thought of nothing except bilberries and scooping.

I could feel years of accumulated urban tension and stress gradually melting away from my head, shoulders, muscles, and spirit. I straightened my back. As far as I could see there was nobody but us in this thick forest. I saw Katja and Päivi quietly and single-mindedly scooping berries a few dozen yards away in the hushed forest that seemed to go on forever. I didn't see Raili. She had vanished somewhere in the woods.

In no time, our pickers were full. We emptied the bilberries mingled with a few leaves and pine needles from the pickers into foraging baskets. I stared at the rich gifts. I felt such gratitude and awe. For me, going into the forest to forage berries has triple health benefits: mental, spiritual, and physical. Berries are packed with nutrients, and eating them is linked to lower risks of cancer and other diseases.

Back at Päivi's home, the Marthas showed me how to make berry juice, bilberry soup, and lingonberry porridge. The apparatus Päivi showed me to make juice with was a stackable steamer with a tube coming out of the pot to drain the juice. She showed me some photos of her making juice before the winter. In the pictures were buckets, buckets, and more buckets of wild berries she had picked, and bottles, bottles, and more bottles of freshly steam-squeezed juice cooling on a counter. My eyes and mouth opened wide. I said, "This is not a hobby—this is a small enterprise!" Päivi brought out a big glass jar filled with ruby-red juice and poured it into shot glasses. We toasted to our health and friendship.

Almost everyone I met said they foraged for berries and made fresh juice, jams, and pies, or froze them to last for a long winter. Now I understood it was time-consuming, hard work, and a way of life. The whole process must give Finnish people a huge sense of accomplishment. Best of all, this "national sport" of foraging was a complete immersion of one's body and soul in pure nature.

Drinking tea and enjoying a homemade berry pie, Karelian pies, artisanal cheese made by their neighbor, and fresh berries, I asked the women what nature—gardens, mushrooms, berries, and forests—means to them.

Päivi explained how the forest is a foundation of her daily life, "It's so nice to go to the forest. For fresh air, and relaxing. I walk my dog in the morning, and she loves to run in the forest." She added, "I love to have vegetables from my garden. I like knowing where they come from."

Päivi's mother, Maire, a longtime Martha in her eighties, with shiny, full silver hair and a glowing face, said, "I started to forage mushrooms when I was about five years old, with my aunt and grandmother." So far, everyone I met in Finland who foraged and fished in the wild told me that they learned the skills from their family growing up. For people like me who are new to Finland, we can learn these skills from the Marthas.

Recalling a mushroom memory, Maire beamed and said, "One year we had very good months for mushrooms. My husband and I were in woods picking mushrooms for two and a half months. We did everything together. We went foraging together. We enjoyed the silence together." She smiled and said, "I feel huge joy in the forest!"

"Foraging in forests heals your soul," explained Päivi. "Why? Quietness is important. I need to be quiet, to be by myself, and to be only with my own head. I need to be alone. In working life, you need to be social, go to meetings and talk, and so on. After a long day at the office, you need your time to have space, quietness, no other people, nor noises. The quietness gives you the energy to go back to work."

Raili chimed in, "Yes, you solve your problems while in the woods." Päivi said, "After a fifteen-minute walk in a forest, your head is clear."

I looked around the table and asked, "Isn't it universal? That everyone needs quietness?"

Päivi hesitated. "I don't know. So many people live in cities."

Katja said, "They just don't know what they're missing."

We all looked at each other in quiet agreement.

House on the Edge of Forever

ONE DAY I TRAVELED TO Ilomantsi, a village on the Russian border, to meet a legendary Martha by the name of Maija-Liisa and her husband, Pekka.

Katja and I were joined by Eeva, a leader of the North Karelian Martha Organization. Katja calls her a "Super Martha." Every time I visited the Martha office in Joensuu to join an activity, Eeva was there orchestrating events. She lived a couple of blocks south of our apartment on Kirkkokatu (Church Street).

When I met her in the car, Eeva was sporting short platinum hair and knitting a sock. She said she could knit one sock one-way on the train from Joensuu to Helsinki, thus a pair of socks round-trip. She knitted while chatting with us on the drive to Ilomantsi.

Katja and Eeva told me that our host in Ilomantsi, Maija-Liisa, was a woman in her late sixties who joined the Marthas when she was in her twenties, was one of the most active and beloved Marthas in North Karelia, and was considered to be a goddess of home cooking. As a career church chef in her village of Ilomantsi, she presided over the food served at countless weddings, funerals, and church events.

Maija-Liisa and Pekka lived in a house on a hill close to the clearly marked but lightly guarded "forbidden zone" between Finland and Russia, between East and West, offering a sweeping view of the surrounding forests and lakes. The exterior of their wooden house was painted in the traditional falu red and white window frames familiar to many cottages and barns in Finland. The warm and comfortable interior was built with natural woods, with bright light pouring in from all directions.

The hills and swamp-like boglands of this wilderness area was home to bears, lynxes, wolverines, elk, and wolves who cross back and forth across the Finland-Russia border, but if an unauthorized human is caught doing this, the penalties are high on either side. Recently, I learned, one bear visited Maija-Liisa's garden at 10:00 P.M. sharp every night to munch on her dandelions.

I barely took three steps into Maija-Liisa's house when she embraced me in a vigorous, prolonged bear hug, as her beaming, lumberjack-sturdy husband, Pekka, looked on. So much for the stereotypical Finnish stand-offishness.

She beckoned me to her oven-warmed wooden kitchen, which was brightly illuminated by the sun and brimming with pots, pans, juicing apparatus, a windowsill lined with jars full of traditional Karelian bounty from the forest, like pine needles, dried mushrooms, berry powders, and *koivun-mahla* (a distillation of sap dripping from birch trees) locally respected as a healthful potion. A giant circular, multitray food dehydrator whirled and hummed in the corner of the kitchen. The kitchen was like a miniature factory.

"I know many recipes," Maija-Liisa explained to me with twinkles in her eyes, "and they are all in my head." With this, she reminded me exactly of my mother, Chizuko, in Tokyo, who is a master of Japanese home cooking and never consults a written recipe. "Everybody knows that two servings of berries are good for your health," Maija-Liisa declared, and she then explained how berries make their way into many of her culinary creations, including smoothies, yogurt, pies, and multigrain bread.

Ilomantsi, located at the easternmost point of the continental European Union, has a special place in the Finnish national soul, as the area was a rich source of poetry and folklore for Elias Lönnrot when he wrote the *Kalevala*, his collection of epic poetry, and the *Kanteletar*, his lesser-known volume of traditional Karelian and Finnish folk songs, hymns, and ballads.

"Maija-Liisa is a huge influence and inspiration for all the Marthas," Katja told me. When I learned of her history, I understood why. Decades ago, Maija-Liisa and the women of the Martha Organization were quiet heroes of a campaign that transformed the physical health of the Finnish nation and saved tens of thousands of lives. Maija-Liisa helped spearhead the rescue. In 1972 a young doctor named Pekka Puska came to the region on a government mission to stop a mass killer.

With a crash education program called the North Karelia Project, he did it—with the crucial help of the Marthas.

The killer was cardiovascular disease, which struck North Karelian men at a ferocious rate, more than any other region in the world. The men were victims of unhealthy life-style patterns that saw half the men smoke and consume a diet that was grossly imbalanced in favor of excessive consumption of meat, saturated fat, sodium, and alcohol, with relatively few plant-based dishes. It was, in part, a product of the trauma of World War II, after which the Finnish government gave many returning veterans their own farmsteads. But since many of the veterans were not experts on farming, they switched to raising pigs and cows instead, and their eating patterns narrowed down to meat, milk, butter, eggs, and not much else.

The result, according to journalist Emily Wittingham, were days "filled with the haze of cigarette smoke—a habit picked up during service—the briny smell of salted meats from the pigs, the heavy aroma of fatty cream and butter from the cows, and the eye-watering sting of alcohol numbing the psychic scars of war." One Karelian resident called it a lifestyle doomed by the "curses of the borderland."

By the 1960s, far too many Karelian men were dying young. In the old days, before the war, many houses in Finnish Karelia had a cellar to store vegetables like carrots and potatoes. Onions were always on the oven, and mushrooms were fried. Berries were made into jam, desserts, or dried. But after the war, when men were encouraged to eat more vegetables, they said they "don't eat rabbit foods."

The Martha chapters included many rural housewives who were sick of seeing their men die young. When Dr. Puska came to town to educate the population about risk factors and lifestyle changes to improve health, the Marthas enthusiastically volunteered to help spread the word. Maija-Liisa's leadership and energy became an inspiration to the project. She and the Marthas decided to focus on their most promising potential ally: Karelian women, who were usually in charge of home life and food preparation. They fanned out to homes and community meetings in the province to help Dr. Puska and his team sponsor "longevity parties," kitchen and fireside chats, posters and leaflets, media campaigns, and meetings with food producers and farmers. They even produced early reality TV programs that pitted village against village in competitions to slash cholesterol counts and smoking rates. Local doctors, nurses, and teachers pitched in to hammer away at a few simple messages—stop smoking, reduce sodium and saturated fat, eat less meat and more produce.

Behind the scenes, the Marthas and their allies among Karelian mothers and housewives quietly applied healthy tweaks to their home cooking that were so subtle that their families barely noticed. The traditional version of North Karelian stew, for example, usually had three ingredients: water, salt, and pork. Now, some of the pork was switched out in favor of carrots, rutabagas, and potatoes. The new recipe caught on, and was nicknamed "Puska's stew." Local meat producers added a mushroom filler to their sausages in favor of less salt and pork fat, and customers liked it so much that sausage sales increased. Local seasonal berry products, previously enjoyed only during the short summer berry season, were made available year-round with new freezing and distribution systems. Fruit consumption boomed.

Soon, North Karelia's health stats for blood pressure, cholesterol, and smoking were shifting in the right direction. By its fifth year, the North Karelia Project was so successful that it was expanded to the entire nation. Within four decades, Finland saw its heart-disease deaths among middle-aged men drop by 80 percent, life expectancy for men jumped by 11.6 years, and the project became a global model for effective public health policy. Maija-Liisa and the Marthas had staged a rescue operation with Dr. Puska that saved the lives of hundreds of thousands of men and their family members.

On the day of our visit, Maija-Liisa's husband, Pekka, offered to take me berry picking while the "Queen Marthas" held a business meeting. We ventured to a swampy spot a few miles away and went in search of *Lakka* (cloudberries, *Rubus chamaemorus*). They are among the world's most nutritious foods, packed with antioxidants, vitamins, minerals, polyphenols, omega fatty acids, and carotenoids. We were briefly attacked by a swarm of large horseflies, which are common in Finland in the summer, but I was prepared: I had bug repellent in my pocket.

"I love this little micro universe of berries!" I exclaimed as I filled up my bucket. "I could spend the whole day here. It's beautiful." I added, "Berry picking is a great workout. You're bending, walking, and hiking."

"Yes," said Pekka.

"When is the high season for cloudberries?" I asked.

"Two weeks ago, at the end of July," said Pekka. Gesturing toward a lake that was very close to the Russian border, he said, "There's the island over there where I'm from. I used to row two kilometers each way at age six every day to go to school. In wintertime, I cross-country skied to school."

As we were walking into their house, Pekka handed me the bucket full of cloudberries and said, "You present this to Maija-Liisa. She will be so happy." I looked at him and nodded. She greeted us at the door, lit up with joy at the sight of the berry bucket, and enveloped me in another great bear hug, as Pekka beamed at us.

We sat down at the dining table. First Maija-Liisa poured a clear liquid from a glass bottle filled with young spruce buds into crystal shot glasses. Pekka said they'd picked the spruce buds earlier in the year and infused them in vodka, creating an aperitif. We raised our glasses with the Finnish toast, "*Kippis!*" It had an evergreen-citrus flavor.

On the table was a pitcher of a light orange-pink beverage, which was homemade rhubarb-lemon-birch-sap juice. The birch sap was collected from trees in the backyard. Maija-Liisa laid out a cornucopia of mouthwatering dishes for lunch, like homemade blueberry-bilberry-coconut pie, chanterelle pie, berry multigrain bread, garden salad, and smoked *muikku* (vendace, *Coregonus albula*) with dill. All were delicious and fresh, and most of the ingredients had been picked that morning or in the last day or two.

When we all finished eating, there was much food left on the plates, and Maija-Liisa and Pekka said, "Please eat more." I asked if I could take home two pieces of fish, bread, and chanterelle pie for William and our son. They sent me home with a whole meal for three people in a container, plus a tub of the cloudberries we'd picked.

After lunch, Pekka gave us a tour of their property. One section was an herb and vegetable garden, and another was a fruit tree orchard. He proudly showed me rows of rich green chard, kale, dill, cabbage, and onions. Gigantic leaves grew around broccolis and cucumbers. A few feet away were flower beds. In a wooden greenhouse, I spotted the edible flowers Maija-Liisa used to garnish the salad, a variety of herbs, and cherry tomatoes for lunch.

In another section was Pekka's outdoor smoker-grill, a black box with a chimney attached to it. He lifted the lid open to show me the inside. At the bottom were charcoals, and a rack above them to place foods. He explained that this was where he smoked the *muikku* fish we had for lunch.

Maija-Liisa came out barefoot. We walked over to a spruce. Holding a low branch to show me tips of the leaves, she explained, "May is the best season for young spruce buds," which she infuses in spirits. She led me to one of the birch trees from which they collected sap that was used in the rhubarb-lemon-birch-sap juice that we had with lunch. Birch sap, or "forest milk," is a clear, slightly cloudy liquid popular in Finland, Russia, Canada, Japan, and Korea and used as a folk medicine for a variety of ailments. It's a power drink rich in amino acids, minerals, enzymes, proteins, anti-oxidants, vitamins B and C, sugar, and betulinic acid, which is anti-inflammatory, antiviral, and heart-healthy.

Maija-Liisa brought out a pitcher of birch sap and glasses. We sat around a picnic table sipping the juice from a tree, which tasted clean, refreshing, and slightly sweet. After saying good-bye, we stopped at the Hermanni Winery in Ilomantsi, the oldest winery in Finland. They produce sparkling wines, berry wines, liqueurs, spirits, and juices made of local currants and berries. The product names are in the Karelian language, and the label designs are inspired by old embroidery traditions in Karelia. We each bought a couple of bottles. Eeva bought jumbo bottles of juices, which the shopkeeper placed in two big bags.

When we approached the Martha office in Joensuu at the end of our trip, I asked Eeva, "How are you going to carry the juices home?"

She said, "I have a bike. I parked it in front of the office."

"You can't carry them on a bike!" I exclaimed, genuinely worried for her safety. "How are you going to keep your balance with the two heavy bags hanging from the bike? You'll fall over! Let me help you take them home."

"I've done it many times," said Eeva, cool as a cucumber. She got out of the car and hugged me good-bye. She grabbed the impossibly bulky juice bags, tied one on each side of the back seat over the rear tire, hopped on her bike, and peddled off.

When I got home, my head was still spinning, my stomach was full and happy, and my heart was practically singing from our visit.

The journey was positively surreal, like a beautiful dream from which I didn't want to wake up.

Temple of the Forest

Among all their marvels, trees are good listeners. They stand silently and courteously, holding space for all our thoughts—the happy ones and the sad ones. They've learned mercy, they've earned wisdom, from observing life unfold. They've seen and heard it all. Sometimes, they will let the wind chime in. Leaves will whisper. Branches will nod. Birds will offer their good sense. Beetles will poke their curious heads out of cracked bark and damp soil. But the trees, unperturbed and dignified, will keep listening to our stories, even before we put them into words.

—MARIANNA POGOSYAN, PhD,
LECTURER IN CULTURAL PSYCHOLOGY

IN 1944, A YOUNG FINNISH woman fell in love.

The subject of her affection was a Karelian farmer by the name of Paavo. The attraction, she explained to a friend, was simple: "I can't resist him—he has eyes like Jesus."

The two were married, and they spent the rest of their lives together on a farm they called Paateri (boat) in the Karelian forest near the lakeside town of Lieska, about sixty miles northeast of Joensuu.

The woman was Eva Ryynänen, and she became a giant in the pantheon of Finnish artists. Her main medium was trees, especially her favorite, pine trees, whose light color she thought reflected the Nordic character.

One day I visited her sprawling studio in the woods. I was astonished by what I saw—a symphony of images large and small, all of them hand-carved from wood, some built into the walls and doors and curved, fluid furniture of her studio and house, of dreams, shapes, characters, angels, infants and children, animals, flowers, nature, and country people.

At the age of eighteen, when Eva was a cowhand on her father's property in a town in central Finland, she carved a striking, intricate wooden sculpture out of a single piece of an aspen tree and called it *The Seven Brothers on a Boulder*. It was inspired by the 1870 literary classic *Seitsemän veljestä* (*Seven Brothers*) by Aleksis Kivi, considered to be a national author of Finland.

The sculpture depicts the misfit, trouble-prone brothers stranded on a boulder in despair while confronted by an angry bull. With the sculpture, Eva won admittance to the prestigious Ateneum school of the Art Association of Finland, along with a cash prize that enabled her to live in Helsinki for a year and a half while moonlighting as a house cleaner.

Unimpressed with the Helsinki art scene, Eva retreated with her true love, Paavo, to their little farm in North Karelia, where they sold milk for thirty years, while in her spare time Eva indulged her passion for sculpting wood. They hand-built a little sauna hut to live in, then expanded with a barn, a house, and an art studio. All the time, Paavo was in awe of his wife's talents. Eva, it turns out, was a self-taught artist, engineer, industrial designer, and toolmaker. "The land is my source," she once explained, "Man is one with nature."

Eva received her first commission for a work to be displayed in a church in 1953. One day, Paavo announced that he had sold the cows, and from that day forward, Eva should devote her life full-time to her passions as an artist. With her husband's support, she experienced her break-through professional triumph as an artist at the age of fifty-nine, in 1974, when a one-person exhibition of her work was unveiled at the Amos Anderson Art Museum in Helsinki. One day in the 1970s, the president of Finland asked if he could pay her a visit, but Eva sent word that she was too busy to see him.

From what I could see as I wandered around her house and studio, Eva seemed completely possessed by the fires of creativity, and it was easy to believe that she channeled some divine power through her fingertips. She once explained that she saw forms hidden inside trees, and felt the wood itself was her negotiating partner and guide as she worked to liberate her visions.

Eva created some five hundred major works of art in her studio over the decades, usually wooden sculptures made from a single piece of wood with no cross-beaming or joined pieces, forged with tools she'd made herself. She specialized in church art, and her creations made it to houses of worship around Finland, and eventually to Sweden, Norway, Germany, Russia, Switzerland, Austria, Italy, Canada, Cuba, Egypt, the United States, and Japan. She felt a deep spiritual connection to wood, and saw it as a medium of the cosmos provided by God. But Eva found it difficult to create sculptures of Christ's crucifixion, explaining that the process made her "suffer for mankind's evil," while "in my heart shines a gentle culture of the sun, where love prevails, not war." Eva passed away in 2001, and her beloved Paavo died three months later. They left their house like they were coming back soon, the kitchenware spread out and their clothes left hanging on pegs on the wall.

A truly stunning creation is her most renowned work, *Paaterin Kirkko* (Paateri Church), finished in 1991, a structure she and Paavo built right on their property as a gift to the community. The church's altar is fashioned from the roots of an immense tree called the Spruce of Karelia from the village of Ruokolahti that was struck by lightning. The church is often used for weddings, and in a mischievous touch, Eva designed the bench in the front row for the bride's mother-in-law to be especially uncomfortable.

According to the scholar Thomas A. DuBois, "each of the church's fourteen pews is carved whole from its own red pine trunk, sanded to a glossy texture and then ornamented with decorative floral patterns." The floor of Paateri Church, he explained, "is made from crosscut sections of pine trunk combined with droplet-shaped pieces of pine, surrounded by a mastic of sawdust, woodchips, and glue, a refinement of a very pragmatic flooring Eva first developed for use in her studio, here elevated to the level of high art."

I stood spellbound inside Eva Ryynänen's church and realized what it was.

It was a Temple of the Forest, a hymn to the spiritual powers of nature.

Woman of Passion

"Do you want to eat, drink, take a sauna, or have sex?"

According to the most powerful Karelian female politician in history, this is how the earthy, sensual countrywomen of Karelia traditionally greet their husbands when they come home.

She prefers the last option first.

Her name is Riitta Uosukainen. She is, by any measure, a political superwoman.

As Finland's education minister in the early 1990s, she was a key force in pushing through reforms that created what is today widely hailed as one of the best, most efficient childhood education systems in the world.

She then became the formidable, fiercely outspoken Speaker of Finland's Parliament for nine years, during a time when Finnish women captured the offices of prime minister, defense minister, and foreign minister, and one third of the seats in Parliament, and she mastered the arts of political combat and compromise, second in power only to the president. As Speaker of Parliament, Riitta dealt face-to-face with Vladimir Putin, the president of neighboring Russia, who in photos of their encounters gazes at her like she is the boss and he is a meek intern. She is one of only eight people ever to have received the nation's highest civilian award, Counselor of State.

Riitta is a master politician of regal bearing and fiery passions, a woman who was described by one journalist as an "unguided ballistic missile." When she heard this, she roared with laughter and said, "Why have only one flight path?" Her political identity, she explained, is that of "a radical, liberal, dynamic conservative." She explained, "My temper is very Karelian. We speak very much and very quickly. And Karelian women speak perhaps more than anyone else in Finland."

When Riitta's memoir was published in 1996, demand was so high that the publisher could barely print books fast enough. That's because, instead of focusing on historical or legislative minutiae, she laid out her emotions on the page, holding forth on people she loves, people she hates, and the secret to her success: sex.

"When things are good in bed, then they are good in general," she pointed out. "I really believe this and I am so sorry that all women do not experience this joy although they have a man, or several, in their lives." She added, "Eroticism, after all, is the power of life and gives power to work." To put it clearly, this is a woman who loves to have sex with her husband. She revealed her passions for him, a retired lieutenant colonel in the Finnish Army named Toivo, in a series of love rhapsodies she printed in her book:

Thank you for that wonderful weekend, for all
the love and pleasure you gave me, the fabulous
moments. The water bed was marvelous—it did not
squeak. And what tidal waves there were when we
made love.

Ah, youth. What a blessed life we had. We made
love so many times and each time I was reduced to
being only breasts, thighs and my sex. Our jobs separated us for a few days, but this did not affect the
statistics too much. Weariness and age have a bit.
But if the signal is alight, I am ready. What signal?
A hint of aftershave or talc, a smell coming from
the forest, a breeze touching clothing, a brushing
against, a glance, a caress, spinning around. All
extraordinary signs so delicious to interpret. The
semiotics of the bedroom.

Take me and I will tremble. You are an officer
and gentleman, a royal-blue archer, the sun of my
life. You know how to be tender and savage, strong
and respectful. You know to make me come. I still
feel your presence inside me.

Remember when we were students? The foot
of the bed broke and we fell on to the floor next to
the old radio set and we laughed like mad. Once the
shops opened, I ran and bought another foot and a
lock for the door. I could never live with a man with

whom I could not laugh in bed. I cry a lot, but tears
have no place in our love life. Instead we laugh!

In a country where politicians are expected to be as dignified and reserved as Lutheran pastors, Riitta's lusty revela-
tions shocked and enraged stuffy politicians—but according
to her, delighted many regular Finns. "When I went on a
book-signing tour, people queued by the hundreds to see me,"
she recalled. "They were like plugging in for electricity." The
book earned her the nickname "Fluttering Flamethrower."
She remembered, "Finnish commentators wanted to kill me
politically, but I was just honest about where I get my power
from and what a great life I have had together with my
husband."

When Riita spoke with me from her house in the woods
in her hometown of Imatra in South Karelia, she was in her
late seventies and technically retired. She was moving a bit
slower than usual, since the week before she had broken her
foot while charging around the marble steps of the magnificent Art Deco Finnish Parliament building in Helsinki. But
her schedule was packed year-round, and she was still barn-
storming the country: attending ceremonies, writing columns,
and giving speeches.

In the case of Riitta Uosukainen, one of the most powerful
lawmakers in her nation's history, her own powers come not
only from the life forces of love and sex but from the woods
of Karelia. "It is a joy to live and work here," she told me. "The
trees are wonderful. The forests, lakes, and nature—they have
made me what I am."

Strong women like Uosukainen have been a pillar of Finland ever since the dawn of history and the myth of the huntress Tellervo, the Finnish goddess of forests and daughter of the forest god Tapio, the protector of cattle. The naked, spear-tossing Tellervo was immortalized in a statue created by the sculptor Yrjö Liipola in central Helsinki in 1929. In Finnish mythology, all living things are protected by the Forest Mother, she is assisted by a team of female guardian-spirits, and Earth is populated with female deities, or "mother spirits."

Not far from Riitta Uosukainen's cottage, on the western side of Lake Saimaa, at a place called Astuvansalmi, is a UNESCO World Heritage site that's believed to be one of the first settlements in Finland. On the side of a sheer cliff there is a series of red ochre Stone Age rock engravings dating to 3800–2200 B.C. that are still visible today. Among the images of people, animals and boats, one stands out, featuring a female figure posing triumphantly after firing her bow at an elk. The prominence of the "Lady With the Bow" in this cradle of Finnish pre-history suggests that she may be a renowned goddess, a shaman, or a master hunter, or perhaps all three. In one of the first written glimpses of the mystery-shrouded tribes of northern Europe, the Roman historian Tacitus in 98 B.C. described the females of the "wild and horribly poor" tribe known as the Fenni, or the possible precursors of both the modern Finns and Finland's Indigenous Sámi people, as assertive and empowered: "The same hunt provides food for men and women alike; for the women go everywhere with the men and claim a share in securing the prey."

According to the Kurdish-Swedish author Nima Sanandaji, the gender egalitarianism typical of modern Nordic cultures can be traced back to the Viking era, when women had strong positions in society. "During the transition to the modern age," he wrote in *U.S. News & World Report* in 2020, "Nordic societies were among the first to give women formalized right to property, to tear down legislative barriers that stopped women from taking professional occupations and also to introduce true democracy by extending the right to vote to both genders." He added that there is also evidence that women in early Nordic societies could inherit property and land, participate in civic affairs, and get a divorce.

When I spoke to the Karelian political titan Riitta Uosukainen, there was one question I had to ask her. "Why is it that today, Finnish women have such a strong position in society—how did this happen?"

She explained, "Finnish women have always been strong; they've worked the fields, tamed the animals, and run the households." As Johanna Kantola, professor of gender studies at Tampere University, once said, "Finnish women's participation in the labor market has always been high. The country industrialized quite late, in the 1960s, and until then women and men were together working in farms and agriculture."

Riitta Uosukainen had one more explanation for the relatively strong position of Finnish women in society.

"The men, you see, are very clever."

"What do you mean?"

She said, "Our men give big value to women. The men are clever because they know it is much easier and better for men to give space and possibilities to women. Together, men and women have worked and made this society a success. Men and women honor each other as partners. That's most important."

"When women have power," she declared, "the men benefit and the nation benefits."

This made perfect sense to me—but I wondered why much of the rest of the world didn't know it yet.

The Lakeland

The daughters of the Sun, Moon, Great Bear, Polar-star, and of the other heavenly dignitaries, are represented as ever-young and beautiful maidens, sometimes seated on the bending branches of the forest-trees, sometimes on the crimson rims of the clouds, sometimes on the rainbow, sometimes on the dome of heaven.

—JOHN MARTIN CRAWFORD, PREFACE
TO THE FIRST ENGLISH TRANSLATION
OF THE *KALEVALA*, 1888

THERE ARE MUSHROOM QUEENS ALL over Finland.

One of them runs the nation's oldest hotel, which is nestled on a ridge near the city of Savonlinna on the banks of Lake Saimaa, Finland's largest body of water, in the Lakeland district of Finland, which borders both North and South Karelia.

She is Saimi Hoyer, a television personality and former
Finnish fashion model who is both a Martha and the owner
and proprietor of the elegant boutique Hotelli Punkaharju.
She spent her childhood summers at a family cottage nearby.
Like so many Finnish people, Saimi is intensely passionate
about nature, and sharing that passion with others. I visited
her one afternoon at the peak of mushroom season.

The hotel was established by Tsar Nicholas I in 1845 as a
forest ranger's lodge with guest rooms, and over time it transformed into Punkaharjun Valtionhotelli (Punkaharju State
Hotel). After its private ownership changed a couple of times,
Saimi bought and restored the property in 2016, to preserve
the building and its history and heritage.

The exterior of the hotel was painted in pale pink, and
borders and window frames were painted in white. Each
guest room has a nature theme—like Nectar, Crane, Dew, and
Dragon Fly—and is furnished with unique pieces handpicked
by Saimi. There was a mushroom-shaped lamp and mushroom art on a wall. One of Saimi's favorite places in the hotel is
the rocking chair terrace that faces a lake. Typical guests, she
explained, were couples who are forty-plus, women's clubs,
and people who love good design, architecture, and nature.

In 2017, the hotel was the scene of a summit meeting
between Russian president Vladimir Putin and Finnish president Sauli Niinistö. The two leaders discussed world affairs,
then boarded the SS *Saimaa* to attend a dinner and an opera
performance by the Bolshoi Theatre at nearby Olavinlinna
Castle. The castle was founded in 1475 to defend the Swedish-
Finnish eastern border, and today is the biggest operatic stage

in the region and host to the acclaimed Savonlinna Opera Festival, which draws tens of thousands of music lovers to the region each summer.

As Saimi served me and my Martha friends an exquisite multicourse mushroom dinner garnished with locally harvested produce, fish, and wild herbs, she explained, "Our guests can enjoy foraging expeditions, fishing, sauna retreats, mountain bikes, Nordic walking poles, standing-paddle boards, canoes, and rowboats." She added, "Events include talks by docents who are familiar with history of Punkaharju."

My favorite dish was *metsäsieni marenkileivos* (forest mushroom meringue). It was chanterelle puree sandwiched between two smoky, light beige meringue puffs. I gently picked it up and took a bite. It was so delicate that it melted in my mouth with earthy, peppery flavors.

"This is nature's most beautiful amusement park!" Saimi exclaimed, echoing the opinion of the nineteenth-century Finnish journalist Zacharias Topelius, who declared Punkaharju as Finland's most beautiful landscape. Not far away, vast armadas of stately forested islands floated on the endless, tranquil lakes that flowed into Lake Saimaa.

If you look very closely, you might spot an endangered and very shy Saimaa ringed seal, a remnant of the Ice Age that improbably survives today in the lakeland of Finland.

A Tokyo Kitchen in Finland

To THANK MY NEW MARTHA "sisters" for their hospitality, I offered to stage a public demonstration of Japanese home cooking at their storefront headquarters on the city square in Joensuu.

My idea was that you could combine healthy aspects of both the Finnish-Karelian and Japanese food patterns that families could enjoy. I titled the evening "Tokyo Kitchen in Your Home Now!" with the description, "Start the winter by introducing one of the most delicious, healthiest diets on Earth—the Japanese diet—into your family meals. Over the last forty years, millions of people in Japan have participated in what amounts to the biggest de facto longevity and anti-obesity experiment of all time. They have discovered how to conquer obesity and live longer than every other nation in the world. Join us for a fun delicious evening. And take home mouthwatering recipes!" Our eight-year-old son and his school buddy handed out leaflets on the town square to spread the word.

The Tokyo Kitchen event quickly sold out. Proceeds were going to the North Karelian Martha Organization as my gratitude for their hospitality to me, and the more attendees we had, the more money we would make. On the day of the event, the weather was miserable and I thought many people wouldn't come. But every single person came—some arrived early, and no one was late.

The Martha kitchen was equipped with industrial cooking islands, perfect for meal preparation and group demonstrations. I explained Japanese table settings and food patterns, and showed how easy and fun it was to prepare a typical Japanese home-cooked meal, including *dashi* (Japanese cooking stock), short-grain sushi-style rice, miso soup with tofu and vegetables, stir-fried vegetables, tender spinach with sweet sesame dressing, and *gyoza* dumplings. I found most of the ingredients I needed from local supermarkets, which are of a very high quality in Finland, with some ingredients shipped up from a Japanese specialty store in Helsinki.

The only thing I couldn't find anywhere was *gyoza* dumpling wrappers. I turned to Jarkko, a nutritionist who was helping me prepare the foods. "I chose dumplings for the menu because they are cousins of Karelian pies," I told him. "I believe you can make dumpling wrappers because you know how to make Karelian pie shells. Could you use wheat flour instead of rye, and make a smaller diameter, about ten centimeters?" He nodded. In typical Finnish "strong, silent, and reliable" style, Jarkko went to work and created perfect dumpling wrappers.

The audience sampled the food, asked questions, and seemed delighted with our cross-cultural food experiment, and the Marthas sent everyone home with goodie bags of authentic Japanese ingredients.

Primeval Forest in Eno

ANNIKA WAS A JOURNALIST WHO wrote a story on the Japanese food event in the local newspaper. Being a journalist, she was filled with insider intelligence about the latest local and national happenings, and once we started talking, it seemed there was no stopping. I asked her many questions about foraging, nature, and social, cultural issues of the moment, and she taught me a lot.

One late summer day, Annika invited me to join her and her husband, Miika, an experienced forestry specialist finishing his masters degree at the University of Eastern Finland, on a hike in a protected forest in Eno, about an hour drive from Joensuu. While over 70 percent of Finland is covered by forest, protected and old-growth forests are relatively rare, and hundreds of years of timber-industry harvests mean that most of the country's forests are young. Environmentalists warn that this makes for more fragile forests, less biodiversity, and more endangered wildlife.

The couple lived deep in the woods, and mostly foraged and hunted for their food, living the wilderness-to-table lifestyle. The protected forest we entered was thick and, like many Finnish forest landscapes, completely random, with no trails or signs. You really need an experienced local guide to keep you on the right track.

When I asked what I should pack for lunch, Annika said, "We may find berries and mushrooms too. We can also make a fire and have tea or coffee there. Of course, Finns grill sausages whenever possible."

Gray and green shades of perfectly straight trees stretched to the sky, and giant fallen branches leaned diagonally on neighboring tree trunks. Different-size trees lay fallen on top of each other, and on the ground, mosses grew all over them. The scenery overflowed with short berry bushes, shrubs, varying lichens, moss, fallen brown leaves, pine needles, and cones covering uneven grounds. Brown mushrooms were sprinkled here and there, and stubby-short tree stumps were capped with vegetation.

Deeper into the woods, Miika reached into a cluster of short ferns on the ground, and pulled one out with its woody root (rhizome). He took out a pocket knife and shaved off the outer layer, revealing a bright green inner tube. He sliced a portion, and handed it to me and another piece to his wife. She said, "Taste it." I chewed it and tasted a sweet, woody flavor. Annika asked, "Doesn't it taste like licorice?" It was common polypody (*Polypodium vulgare*), often used in candies. We agreed that it made a good chewing snack while we walked through the woods. Then Annika spotted a few feet over our heads a dark, rough-surfaced growth protruding from a birch tree, pushing and peeling its bark. It was chaga (*Inonotus obliquus*), the source of the life-prolonging elixir I had enjoyed with Päivi the Mushroom Queen.

Further on, we spotted semicircular caps that looked like horse's hoofs protruded from thin tree trunks. They belonged to a group of fungi called polypores, and their common name is pore fungus (*Fomes fomentarius*).

Annika gently touched a foot-long light grayish green tassel hanging from a tree branch. She explained, "This is beard moss, a type of lichen. When we see them, we know the air is pristine." They were growing on many branches all around us.

We came to a small open field, she pointed to the ground and I saw amber spots. Many of them. Chanterelle mushrooms, treasures of nature. We bent down, picked handfuls, and laid them in a basket, exchanging victory smiles. When we were back in Joensuu, Annika placed all the golden Chanterelles in a brown paper bag and handed them to me to savor with my family.

When Annika originally invited me on this journey, I imagined us picking berries from low bushes and popping them in our mouths as we hiked. I imagined Miika making a fire and grilling sausages, and boiling water for tea. Our dining room decor would be thick evergreens with sunlight streaking through gaps between their trunks and branches. Above our heads would be both puffy and wispy clouds moving slowly across a light blue sky, indicating the passing of the summer and the arrival of autumn days. Under our boots would be a thick, uneven velvety cushion of mosses and fallen pine needles. We would drink tea out of wooden cups called *kuksa* that the Indigenous people Sámi of northern Finland's Lapland traditionally hand-carved out of birch burls.

And that's exactly what happened. If this wasn't a vision of the ultimate meal from Mother Earth, what was?

A forest is truly a magical place, I kept thinking.

Forest of Darkness and Light

"FOR ME IT FEELS LIKE I won the lottery when I was born as a girl in Finland," Tanja Auvinen, a government official at the Finnish Ministry of Health and Social Affairs, once said. "Our history has shown we can be proud of our achievements, but I also think we have to be vocal and always strive for better. We still have lots of work to do."

Finland is not Utopia, and Finns like Tanja will be the first to point out there is much work to do to improve the position of women in society, and to improve society itself.

There is, in fact, a dark side to Finland, as there is to most societies. I learned that a very grave concern in Finland is domestic violence, a problem that is among the worst in Europe. Finnish legislation on domestic violence and marital rape has been severely inadequate. "This is a paradox: a high level of gender equality also produces an illusion of full equality already existing, and of further policies being unnecessary or excessive," observed activist lawyer and University of Turku law professor Kevät Nousiainen in 2019. "It's assumed that women are perfectly capable of taking care of themselves, and if they are not able to do so, that is unacceptable."

The struggle for gender and social progress in modern Finland could be incredibly difficult at times, and was often forged in conditions of severe poverty and inequality.

One of the original first nineteen female members of the 1907 Finnish Parliament, Maria Raunio, was a widow and single mother of five. When she campaigned for equal rights for children born out of wedlock, Raunio's father, who was a tailor, was abandoned by his wealthy customers, forcing the large family to starve and causing Raunio's children to be sent periodically to live in an alms house. She eventually emigrated to the United States, lost contact with her children, fell into depression and committed suicide.

Before she died, Maria Raunio described a vision she had for the future of her nation: "You shall go and create a new Finland. Build a country of happiness where no unsheltered mother shall shed tears with a bleeding heart but where they see an abundance of food and warmth for their beloved children." In barely a century, her dream-prophesy would largely come true.

Alcohol abuse in Finland has declined in recent years but remains high, echoing a problem common to many societies, especially northern ones with long periods of winter darkness. Social inequality in Finland is on the rise, though it is still very low compared to many other developed nations.

Finland has made strong efforts to welcome immigrants and ethnic and cultural minorities as full members of society, but here, too, its record is far from perfect, and there is much work to be done. Immigrant women and men in Finland face discrimination and underemployment. In Finland's rush to modernity, its Indigenous Sámi population, largely concentrated in Lapland, has suffered disconnections with its traditional way of life, leading to social and health challenges that afflict so many First Peoples.

There is racism in Finland, and even racial violence, in a society that is less culturally diverse than many other European nations. People of Iraqi, Afghan, Russian, Somali, and Roma backgrounds in Finland have been subject to hate crimes, which have been on an overall decline from 2009 to 2018, but sadly persist, and are highest in North Karelia, where we were residents, an economically distressed area with relatively small foreign-background communities.

A 2019 analysis by the European Commission Against Racism and Intolerance reported that in Finland, "racist and intolerant hate speech in public discourse is escalating; the main targets are asylum-seekers and Muslims." Ironically, in the Finnish society that so strongly values and showcases working women, some newly arrived female refugees have felt resented and looked down on if they don't enter the workforce quickly. A 2020 report from the Finnish government's Equality Ombudsman found that four out of five people of African heritage have experienced discrimination in Finland based on the color of their skin. "Racism runs deep also in our society," the report declared. "Our ways of thinking and our modes of action are to a large extent racist even if we do not notice it or are unwilling to admit it."

According to the Finnish-born writer Maryan Abdulkarim, "Sometimes foreign blood is a source of pride in Finland, but this honor unfortunately does not apply to people of Somali origin." In 2019, she wrote, "Over the years, the word 'Somali' has bounced around me in schoolyards, public spaces, in political rhetoric and made news headlines. The word rarely carries a neutral or positive tone. For some Finns, Somali, my actual heritage, is a swear word."

Later that year, in a *Politico* article headlined "Finland is no Feminist Utopia," Abdulkarim wrote of gender progress in Finland not as an accomplished fact but as a work in progress: "Women entered the work force *en masse* following the Winter War—Finland's military conflict with Russia, which lasted from November 1939 until March 1940—to help pay off the country's war debts to Moscow. And they never left. But scratch below the surface and Finnish society is still far from being gender-balanced. Working life was and remains gendered—there are so-called masculine and feminine fields, and, as elsewhere, there is a significant pay gap between men and women who perform the same work." But good news was reported in 2021 by the World Economic Forum in its annual Global Gender Gap Report: "An important area where Finland has improved this year is the increased presence of women in senior and managerial roles, where women currently represent 36.9% of the total, an increase of about five percentage points."

Finally, there are the issues of mental health, which appeared paradoxical to me in a country that ranks as the world's happiest nation, where I met so many outwardly serene, content, and confident people. According to a 2018 report by the Nordic Council of Ministers and the Happiness Research Institute in Copenhagen, about 16 percent of Finnish women aged eighteen to twenty-three and 11 percent of young men say they are "struggling" or "suffering" in life. In 2019, Kirsi-Marja Moberg, who struggled with depression through her twenties, explained to the BBC journalist Maddy Savage, "You almost feel like you don't have the right to be depressed when you're living in a country like Finland where the living standard is so high." Savage reported, "Suicide rates in Finland are half what they were in the 1990s and have reduced across all age groups—a shift which has been linked to a nationwide suicide prevention campaign when things were at their worst, alongside improved treatment for depression," but added that "they remain well above the European average." Perhaps, some think, the "happiest nation" reputation, plus Finns' reluctance to display emotion, makes it difficult for some Finns, especially young men, to identify and seek treatment for depression and other mental health issues.

At the same time, however, Finland has scored tremendous achievements in social progress and gender equality—in politics, education, and society, and especially when compared to other developed nations. The nation recently ranked as number one in the world for educational achievement for women. Women currently account for over half of university graduates in Finland, and the female-to-male workforce participation rate of 88.5 percent, compared with an EU average of 81 percent and with a world average of 65.8 percent.

In the World Economic Forum's 2021 Global Gender Gap Report, Finland ranked behind only fellow Nordic nation

Iceland for having the world's lowest magnitude of gender-based disparities in society, while the United Kingdom
ranked number 23, the United States ranked number 30,
and Japan came in at number 120 out of 156 nations. In 2019,
women won a record 47 percent of the seats in Parliament,
and in 2021 fully half of Finland's government ministerial
posts were held by women.

Homelessness, child poverty, crime, and imprisonment
in Finland are, by global standards, extremely low. Finland's publicly supported childcare, senior care, education,
health care, unemployment insurance, and universal paid
parental leave benefits are among the absolute best in the
world.

The World Economic Forum's global Social Mobility
Report placed Finland at number two (tied with Norway)
after world-topping Denmark in the ability of a child to experience a better life than their parents. Germany and France
came in at number 11 and number 12, respectively; the United
Kingdom ranked number 21; and the United States was
number 27 out of 82 nations. A 2020 analysis of 210 nations
and territories by the nonpartisan Freedom House found
that Finnish, Norwegian, and Swedish citizens enjoy the best
political rights and civil liberties in the world, each scoring a
100 on an index of 100.

There are legislative plans to reform Finland's Trans Act,
a law that currently, and inexplicably, requires those seeking
legal gender recognition to go through years of mental health
screening, and unless they are already infertile, forced

sterilization. "Other than in this one conspicuous policy area," wrote Danny Dorling and Annika Koljonen in their 2020 book *Finntopia*, "Finland's recognition of LGBTQ rights and related policies are very good in the main (although outranked by Norway) and very much better than most countries in eastern, central and southern Europe."

In 2000, Tarja Halonen was elected as Finland's first female president. She went on to serve a full twelve years, a period that also saw Finland's first and second female prime ministers, Anneli Jäätteenmäki and Mari Kiviniemi. In 2007, Finland's cabinet for the first time had more women than men—twelve versus eight.

Contrary to some clichés, Finland is far from being a "socialist" nation, which usually means government interference with the free market, the stifling of investment and business innovation, and limitations on human rights.

In fact, according to the title of a 2019 opinion piece in the *New York Times* by the Finnish-born Anu Partanen and her husband, Trevor Corson, "Finland Is a Capitalist Paradise." Nordic nations like Finland, they wrote, realize that "capitalism works better if employees get paid decent wages and are supported by high-quality, democratically accountable public services that enable everyone to live healthy, dignified lives and to enjoy real equality of opportunity for themselves and their children." They cited a report by J. P. Morgan Asset Management that the Nordic nations are not only "just as business-friendly as the U.S." but also do better on free-market indexes like protecting private property and openness to trade and capital flows. "Everything works" in Finland, according to Partanen and Corson, "Everything is arranged in a way that you don't have to go through a lot of trouble to arrange your life."

If capitalism worked the way it was supposed to, it would look a lot like Finland.

Wave That Flag

I STARTED NOTICING FINNISH FLAGS regularly bursting forth all over the place on a regular basis, then disappearing the next day.

These are really patriotic people, I mused.

The reason, I learned, was no less than twenty-four different Finnish flag days spread through the year, including Culture Day, Literature Day, Summer and Poetry Day, and the Day of Children's Rights. Three are named for accomplished Finnish women. March 19 is Minna Canth—Social Equality Day, named after the nineteenth-century playwright and strong gender-equality advocate; August 9 is designated Tove Jansson—Art Day, named after the creator of the forest-dwelling, mushroom-and-berry-foraging Moomin characters.

The October 1st flag day is known as Miina Sillanpää—Civic Participation Day, to honor the women's rights campaigner who became Finland's first female cabinet minister in 1926. She was born into a peasant family during a national famine in the 1860s; worked in factories as a child laborer; and became a trailblazer in politics, social democracy, and gender rights. She served as a member of the Finnish Parliament for thirty-eight years, and as head of the Servants' Association for nearly fifty years. She was a champion for the rights of working women, and was a leader in establishing *ensikoti*, or shelters for single women and their children.

Today, women like her are a powerful inspiration to Finns in their ongoing national quest for social justice.

Family Outing

SHE CAME OUT OF THE darkness and misty rain, with a two-year-old girl strapped into a bucket on the back of her bicycle.

"So glad you could make it!" she exclaimed.

Her name was Irmeli Mustalahti. She was a world-renowned professor of natural resources governance, and a fellow parent at the university teacher-training lab school, where our eight-year old sons were becoming fast friends, despite the fact that neither boy yet spoke the other's language. Her stately, commanding beauty evoked images by Raphael or Botticelli, and like many Finnish women I was getting to know, her personality seemed suffused in a kind of calm, confident determination, contentment, and serenity.

Maybe they're all blissed out by all the fresh air and the forest, I mused to myself.

Over lunch one day, Irmeli told me, "In my childhood, the forest was my playground. Back then my parents didn't transport me to different hobbies or activities. I started going into the forest alone when I was five years old, to go skiing, hiking, and picking berries and mushrooms. The family cat and dog came with me and watched over me. I only got lost once, and not for long. There's not much to be afraid of in the forest. In Finland, only city folk and politicians are afraid of the forest. Like a lot of Finns, we had lots of trees on our property and they were our 'bank account.' My parents planted, harvested, and sold trees for a living. It provided our family's main income. You learn respect for nature when you look after such a bank account." She added, "I have epilepsy, which can be triggered by stress, so even today the forest is quite important neurologically and psychologically for me, as a place for healing."

Besides being a fellow public school mom and one of my guides to the local customs in Finland, Irmeli was a professor and one of the world's leading social scientists specializing in natural resources governance. The year before, she was honored with the award for social impact by the prestigious National Academy of Finland. She was a globe-trotting expert on the interactions between human beings and nature, and frequently traveled from Joensuu to places like the United Nations in New York, Tanzania, Nepal, Mexico, Mozambique, and Laos to promote collaboration between government, business, youth, and communities on natural resources governance.

On this early autumn night, Irmeli met my family near the city square, and we headed for the festival grounds on the nearby island of Ilosaari in the middle of the Pielisjoki River, where an outdoor movie and music event that she had invited us to was supposed to be starting shortly.

But all through the day, it had been raining. I was surprised the event hadn't been canceled yet. This made little sense.

I asked, "Will they move the show indoors because of the weather?"

"Why, of course not!" Irmeli replied quizzically. "We all have the right clothes on, and remember, as we Finns say, there is no bad weather, only inadequate clothing." Irmeli's son, who had a cold but didn't want to stay at home and miss the fun, sneezed. "What doesn't kill you makes you stronger," noted his mother.

The Finns took these sayings very seriously to the point of sending all the nation's schoolchildren outdoors every day for multiple fifteen-minute outdoor recesses, regardless of the weather, in snow, ice, rain, and temperatures as low as minus 10 degrees Fahrenheit.

Up ahead on the bridge to the island, I saw there were long columns of local couples, families, and groups of friends gamely trudging through the mud and slop toward the event.

When we got there, I couldn't believe my eyes. There were dozens of Finnish men, women, and children, standing contentedly still outside in the open air, in the rain, stoically waiting for a movie to begin on the jumbo screen. To my even bigger surprise, off to the side, a group of naked adults relaxed discreetly while submerged in a small outdoor portable hot tub and sauna on wheels, sipping champagne.

In many parts of the world, weather like this would send people running for shelter. But here in rural Finland, these were perfectly normal conditions in which to take your loved ones—including small children—to watch an outdoor movie.

"This is a short film about the woods and mountains of Koli national park, an hour north of here," Irmeli explained. The movie started, and the majestic opening chords of "Finlandia" by Jean Sibelius boomed through the speakers. The screen revealed the magnificent visuals of Koli.

Around me, the crowd was transfixed. We were standing outdoors in thick mist and rain, fully exposed to the elements, practically swimming in mud, on a little island in the middle of a river—watching a movie about a forest.

I asked Irmeli what the name of the island, Ilosaari, means.

"It is Finnish for 'Island of Joy,'" she smiled.

Of course it's called the Island of Joy, I thought. *That makes perfect sense.*

Light in Total Darkness

By mid-November, Finland was rapidly plunging into its winter abyss of darkness and cold.

Suddenly, the atmosphere of a pleasant Nordic autumn vanished, and shadows and mud slammed into Karelia like a freight train.

I was surprised to learn that many Finns have never fully adjusted to the reality of twilight falling early in the mid-afternoon, and some of them become gloomy at the looming prospect of four months or more of dark, cold days. But I saw many Finns stoically take the winter in stride. Workers commuted to their offices on cross-country skis. Many women walked briskly with Nordic poles.

In a climate like this, one cannot sit and wait for the winter to pass. Life goes on. I watched elderly people use walkers to venture to stores on snowy sidewalks from my kitchen window, providing me encouragement to keep on moving.

I was startled to see hundreds of Joensuu adults and children racing around the ice-packed, snow-packed streets and sidewalks of the city on bicycles, and somehow managing not to wipe out. Half the students in our son's primary school got to school this way, even children as young as seven and eight years old, and they did it in temperatures of minus 10 degrees Fahrenheit. In 2020, just before the COVID-19 pandemic hit, the city would host the annual Winter Cycling Congress, a niche event if ever there was one.

Winter was the time of year when I originally expected to feel miserable, push the eject button, and flee back to New York City. But with the help of my Finnish friends, I felt the opposite: completely relaxed and content in my home in the enchanted forest. The darkness and cold weren't much worse than what I was used to in New York.

Because of the rural setting of the city, the darkness in North Karelia seemed authentic—there were few street lights and little artificial light pollution. In fact, it was pitch black. When I walked to pick up my son at his after school program at 4:30 P.M., I followed the local winter tradition of wearing a neon yellow vest with reflective silver lines across my chest over my winter coat. I knew someone was walking a dog across the street only because I saw a blinking light attached to the dog and the reflective gear of the owner. I noticed bikers only because of their headlights, which are required by law.

This is when I discovered the true meaning of *light*, the vivid effect of precious lights in an absolute darkness, and the significance of a candle service at church. All my life I lived in neon-and-artificial-light-filled cities. Lights over lights, almost canceling each other out. Manhattan was glittered with holiday decorations and lights this time of the year, and the Christmas tree at Rockefeller Center was adorned with fifty thousand lights. The cityscape and the tree were beautiful, but it was a different kind of beauty. Light and darkness in North Karelia were more authentic, and their power seemed sharpened. I came to more fully appreciate the meaning of light, thanks to the pure darkness.

In early December, our family took a train trip to Rovaniemi, the capital of the Lapland district of northern Finland. This required a four-and-a-half hour southbound train ride from Joensuu to Helsinki, then a northbound sleeper car for an all-night train to Lapland, where we saw a stunning display of the Northern Lights and went dogsledding, snow tubing, and reindeer riding at Santa Claus Village on the Arctic Circle. Our son, who turned eight in Finland, had the time of his life. The national public transportation system in Finland is excellent, and trains between major destinations are clean, comfortable, and fast. Our son took advantage of the mini playgrounds and mini libraries installed in the trains for children to enjoy. And we parents enjoyed our time on our own.

As our train sped silently north toward the roof of the world and a rendezvous with the man who Finland has officially anointed as the world's one and only *authentic* Santa Claus, I gazed out the window and pondered the ghostly frozen woods.

This is the real Polar Express, I thought.

Awakenings

I WAS CHANGING. I COULD feel it.

As our six-month sojourn drew to a close, I felt like I was turning into something new. I was becoming Naomi 2.0, a reboot of myself.

December was a time for holiday celebrations and farewells to Finland, and for reflections on sisterhood, motherhood, and navigating the next chapter of my life. This strange land was becoming a part of my soul.

In the summer, when my family and I first landed at this remote, bucolic part of Finland, I was a Tokyo-born woman, a former executive, a wife, and now a full-time stay-at-home mom. I had a New York City–born husband and a seven-year-old boy.

I'd spent my last twenty-five years in New York, the ultimate roller-coaster city of drama, overachievement, self-promotion, and sensory stimulation. That city was an intellectual utopia, with perhaps the world's richest array of museums, concerts, restaurants, art galleries, and global diversity. On many days, I loved it. But it was also, notoriously, a pressure cooker—of noise, stress, and cramped living quarters. The city's hypercompetitive culture extended down to the diaper set, where toddlers and parents engaged in fierce competition for precious slots in elite preschools.

I had lived inside the Manhattan symphony of joy, anger, love, beauty, conflict, relentless competition, and individual achievement for so long that by now it seemed perfectly normal. But it was dawning on me that an entirely different way of life was possible, and in many ways I was starting to admire it more.

Until now, I had been shaped by life in two countries—a childhood and adolescence in Japan, and a college and adult life in the United States. Now, I was living in a sparsely populated Nordic society of lush nature, otherworldly silences, smart, fascinating, rugged, and down-to-earth people, and a radically different social structure from the United States, one built more on community than on competition. Neither structure was perfect, but I realized they had much to learn from each other.

I remember someone telling me that you can't choose your parents as a child, and after spending a few weeks in Finland, I realized that you usually can't choose your society, either. And it can significantly affect who you become and how you live.

I started asking my new local friends if they knew how lucky they were to be born in Finland. They almost always responded "yes," and without prompting would cite great schools, health care, and social and government services as the reason, as well as the relatively low-stress, high-nature lifestyle they enjoyed.

In the United States, the words *welfare state* had become a term of derision, conjuring up images of welfare cheats living on food stamps and driving Cadillacs with stolen government money; but in Finland the phrase was a national badge of honor, signifying compassion and love for all members of society. Over and over, I heard Finnish people repeat mantras like "We've got to watch out for one another," and "We're all in this together" to explain their fiercely communitarian and egalitarian outlook.

I began to realize that in Finland, nature is the ultimate personal luxury. And it was everywhere, available for absolutely anybody to enjoy. I considered the paradox of how one of the world's most advanced societies seemed to value nature as much as the individual accumulation of wealth or property.

This place was changing me as a parent. On the first day that he walked to school by himself at age seven, my husband and I watched our son's tiny figure recede into the horizon on a journey that would take him across eight street crossings, a traffic circle, and two busy main streets. I felt nervous, but also proud, because we both knew he could handle it, like nearly every other child in Finland.

But now I was coming to believe that all public schools should strive to serve all children with excellence and equity and treat teachers as elite professionals, as they do in Finland, which was soon ranked by the *Economist* as the number one school system in the world for preparing children for the future. The public schools are so good that there are almost no private or parochial schools, since demand for them is almost nonexistent.

As our son attended a Finnish public school, I found myself shifting from a "New York Mom," consumed with my child's school performance, sports, and extracurricular activities, to a more laid-back "Nordic-style Mom" approach. I adopted a largely hands-off attitude to school and sports. I trusted his teachers to do a great job, since Finnish teachers are trained as classroom clinicians and researchers with master's degrees in education. They conduct individualized assessments of children's learning every day.

At our son's school and all other Finnish schools, children received a fifteen-minute recess every hour; a hot lunch every day; and small class sizes, including carpentry, cooking, sewing, ethics, and foreign languages, in a school where comfort, confidence, and mutual respect between children and teachers was the prevailing atmosphere. At public schools in New York City, free meals were just being phased in, but in Finland they have been a fact of daily school life since 1943.

Finland is a pioneer and current world leader in the concept of free lunches for all its schoolchildren. "When school offers free lunch, it is also a great opportunity to learn many important life skills," noted the Finnish educator Pasi Salberg. "In Finland, for example, during lunch children learn about nutrition, food in different cultures, and good manners at the lunch table. Most schools have introduced a weekly vegetarian day and have no-waste policies to teach how the food we eat influences the well-being of our planet." The payoff can be huge, as Pasi notes that "a growing amount of research shows school-wide free lunches lead to better academic and health outcomes. A Brookings Institute study in California revealed that students who were offered daily healthy lunch scored higher on state tests, with larger score increases among students who were eligible for reduced price or free lunches. Other research shows that when free lunch is served for all children in school, fewer get repeatedly suspended."

This one relatively small investment in the daily well-being of schoolchildren in Finland contributes to an invaluable return—better health and better learning, in the most equitable school system in the world. According to Sahlberg, the fact that this powerful social innovation has been in place on a national basis for nearly eighty years is largely due to "the hard work and wisdom of women and women's groups since the early twentieth century."

We could and should do much of this in schools in the United States, I thought, *if only American parents, teachers, and policymakers could see this with their own eyes.* After school every day, our son went by himself to a low-cost after-school program that focused on arts and crafts, sports, and outdoor play. At the school, one of his physical education classes consisted of going into the woods with his classmates and trying to find his way around with a map and compass, or orienteering, under the loose supervision of a teacher.

After a few weeks of orienteering in Joensuu, our son knew many shortcuts through forests where I had no idea there were passages. I had usually been walking on well-trod pedestrian paths, never dreaming of venturing into a thick, forested area. One day our son showed me how quickly we could go from Koivuniemen koirapuisto, a park near the mouth of River Pielisjoki, to Linnunlahti, the bay on the other side, by taking a tiny path through the woods.

I was learning the national sports of mushroom and berry picking, and discovering the joys of local Finnish cooking and friendships and attitudes toward life.

At first, it wasn't clear to me why Finland was ranked as one of the world's happiest nations. Outwardly, they didn't look much happier than anyone else. In fact, the default facial expression of many Finns was blank, bordering on morose. But I soon realized that their happiness wasn't a boisterous, slaphappy exuberance, but a deeper sense of serenity and contentment, a feeling that comes from living in a society that is simultaneously super high tech yet profoundly connected to nature, and organized so efficiently that unnecessary day-to-day stress is minimized, and basic social services are among the best of all nations.

This place was changing me. My ideas of success were changing. Instead of individual achievement alone, perhaps real success meant that everyone in the community should succeed to the maximum extent possible. Perhaps we should measure personal success in part by how well-off and how well cared for all the members of society are. Finnish citizens pay significantly higher taxes than Americans, but most Finns see it as a good bargain for everyone, since Finns demand, and receive, a very high standard of government-supported social benefits that are shared equally by everyone, like their schools, creating a better overall society.

My ideas of wealth were changing, too. Instead of money and material possessions, perhaps true wealth includes access to and immersion in pure nature, which this society has in such abundance. Finland is basically one enormous nature park, and even residents of Helsinki live just a short distance from thick forests, pristine lakes, and peaceful hiking trails. True wealth also includes the social wealth of the whole community—health care, child and senior care, education, transportation, and security and sustainability for all citizens. A fuller, more authentic vision of capitalism, I realized, should enable citizens and companies to demand a much higher minimum standard of public services, as is the case in Finland. The bottom lines should be people, quality of life, and well-being—not just money.

My notions of relaxation and luxury were also changing. Many Finns have a summer or weekend cottage on a lake. When I first heard this, I thought it sounded extremely luxurious. But soon I realized that the country was filled with lakes, and it was extremely easy for anyone to have a place on a lake. The cottages are not enormous mansions or villas, but modest, cozy, simple wooden structures with a small kitchen next to a communal eating and sitting area, and a side room or attic for sleeping quarters. Many don't have running water. Family members take turns bringing water from a well. Many don't have electric or gas heating systems—a big oven sits between the kitchen and sitting area fueled by birch, warming the entire cottage. When you come in on a wet or cold day, you just prop your hat, mittens, scarf, and coat over the stove.

A cottage often has a separate sauna house closer to the lake. Year-round, Finns walk from their cottage to sit in a steamy hot sauna. Once they are sufficiently warmed or hot, depending upon their preferences, they step out of the sauna house and jump into the lake, or even roll around in thick snow. Then back to the sauna. And repeat.

Back in New York, and in many other parts of the world, people often complained about inadequate social services and inept politicians. Here in Finland, people felt free to complain, too, but everyone seemed to trust each other and their leaders much more to look out for the common good, and to do the right thing for the community. *Trust* is another cultural mantra in Finland, and that word is often used to describe the most important social bond shared by all members of Finnish society. Maybe, I was realizing, it really is possible to organize a thriving, free market, capitalist democracy that strives to deliver strong social services, freedom, security, and a good life to all of its citizens.

As I transitioned from my childhood and adolescence in Japan and my adult life in the United States to this radically different social structure filled with nature, silence, and inspiring personalities, I could feel my own attitude and personality changing. Now, approaching the end of my family's stay in Finland, I realized I was not the same person I used to be. I had hit the refresh button on my life. My soul was being nourished.

But I still couldn't figure out the secret of this small, faraway nation. Was it a fluke, an oddball, an outlier? In barely one century, how had it achieved so much in gender progress, human rights, happiness, freedom, safety, governance, literacy, rule of law, and many other dimensions? And why was I feeling so, well, *happy* and stress-free here?

Eventually, the answer, or at least part of it, dawned on me. It wasn't something the locals talked about too much, since Finns are famously modest and averse to self-promotion. It wouldn't seem like an unusual idea to them, since it was already baked into their national DNA, but for most of the rest of the world, it was a revolutionary idea.

Now it was starting to make sense.

This country, more than many others, was founded, built, shaped, nurtured, and run—by women.

A Little Piece of Finland in New York

IT WAS TIME TO RETURN to New York.

The Finland chapter of my life seemed to be over.

I was happy to return to Manhattan, where the days seemed much longer in winter than they had in Karelia. *It's all relative*, I told myself. I had a renewed excitement for the city and all the diversity and amenities it offered, which I may not have fully appreciated before spending time in Finland.

But I was soon gripped with an inexplicably fond nostalgia for mushroom hunting. Before we left Joensuu, a group of my Karelian Martha "sisters" had given me a gift supply of hand-foraged, home-dried, vacuum-packed mushrooms to remember them by. Back in New York, I opened a bag, savored the distinctive earthy aroma, and cooked the mushrooms with a few drops of chaga potion. I wondered if there was some group in the New York area, or more likely far away, that was devoted to mushroom foraging.

I typed "mushroom, New York, foraging" into Google. To my surprise, the first result hit the jackpot—New York Mycological Society, cofounded by composer John Cage and other mushroom enthusiasts sixty years ago. This group of devoted mushroom aficionados was based and operated in, of all places, New York City. The site said that their mushroom walk destinations can be reached by public transportation. Incredible. I immediately became a member, and soon joined them for expeditions in Central Park and across New York City parks.

The first mushrooming expedition was on a freezing New Year's Day. I went to the meeting point at 95th Street and Central Park West bright and early, imagining I might be the only person crazy enough to show up. Slowly but surely, over twenty mushroom hunters gathered. Half of them had completed the New Year's Eve four-mile midnight run a few hours earlier. After the walk, the group's then-president and legendary mycologist Gary Lincoff and his wife Irene invited us back to their apartment for a New Year's feast of mushroom soup and other delicacies. Weeks later, there was an annual Morel breakfast followed by a Morel hunt at a secret location. New York never ceased to amaze me.

One day in the early spring, I noticed a poster for a volunteer gardening day tied to a fence of the playground across the street from our apartment on 96th Street, where my husband and I spent countless hours watching our son play with his neighborhood buddies. For all the time I spent in the playground, I barely noticed the fragile flower beds or little patches of greenery surrounding it.

On the volunteer day, I met three longtime gardeners who lived close by. None of their children played in the playground; they were all grown-up. But these women loved to garden, were very knowledgeable about plants, and wanted an attractive park near their homes. They cared about the community. A woman who lived in a brownstone on 95th Street across from the playground had started a local association to beautify the park and recruited these three ladies at around the same time. The founder moved away after some years, but these cofounders stayed.

The little garden in the playground became my backyard, and I became its volunteer guardian and champion in the weeks ahead, supervising tree and garden plantings and refurbishments with the New York City Department of Parks and Recreation. I attended workshops organized by the New York City Parks Foundation. I applied for a grant from the foundation to buy plants for the park working closely with the cofounder gardeners. With the grant, our group purchased azalea bushes and cigarette butt receptacles from a recycling company named TerraCycle, which we mounted on the metal fence facing a sidewalk where smokers tossed their cigarette butts on the way into a subway station. TerraCycle provided mailing labels and prepaid shipment for the recycled cigarette butts we mailed. On their website, we could monitor how many butts we had recycled.

I had created a little piece of Finland for myself in New York City—a personal oasis of sisterhood, volunteerism, and engagement with nature. There was, of course, nothing exclusively Finnish about these things, and the United

States and other nations had them on vast scales, too. But Finland made me better appreciate the things I had in my own backyard.

Finland's forest—and its women—had inspired and changed me in many ways. I had glimpsed the power of nature, sisterhood, and food to nourish the spirit and soul.

I had seen how nature, childhood, and quality family time could be so cherished in an ultra-modern, high-tech society. I saw how young children could be trusted to manage themselves and learn through play, largely on their own. I had joined an entire nation of parents who believed that children should be children, and that childhood should be protected as a time for joy, discovery, and well-being, not stress, competition, and overwork. I learned to relax more as a mother.

Finland made me appreciate more deeply the childhood I had in Tokyo and my adult years in Illinois and New York. Finland made me realize the differences and the similarities of each culture. As the poet T. S. Eliot wrote, "We shall not cease from exploration, And the end of all our exploring, Will be to arrive where we started, And know the place for the first time."

Most importantly, with my husband and my son, I had lived inside a society that was cofounded and co-led by an incredible tribe of strong, brilliant women. They made me appreciate more deeply all the powerful women I knew, and grew up with, and admired, in Japan, the United States, and around the world—and the men who supported them.

Finland made me see that a superbly woman-friendly, child-friendly, mother-friendly, and family-friendly society was actually possible—and real. It was not an impossible dream, but a living, daily reality in a tiny, thriving democracy at the edge of the world. It made me realize that all children, women, and men deserve a society like this—it was perfectly normal, and right.

My Finland journey was nothing short of a revelation to me on the subjects of gender equity and the power of strong, brilliant, confident women to shape society.

Reentering the Workforce

ONCE BACK IN NEW YORK City, it was time for a major transition in my life.

After being a full-time mom, it was time for me to reenter the workforce.

Pre-Finland, I was already hoping to do this, but my time in Finland renewed and strengthened my zeal to get back to a full-time career.

When I became pregnant, I knew I wanted to be a stay-at-home parent for at least the first three years. There is a Japanese saying, "A three year old's soul lasts to 100," which is similar to the saying "What's learned in the cradle is carried to the grave." My mother was a stay-at-home mom, which was typical of the era, and growing up I loved having her at home. I wanted to be there for our child as much as I could when he was an infant and a toddler. A child's growth is miraculous, and I didn't want to miss a second of it. I loved motherhood. Three years turned into five, then seven.

Then after eight years of being a full-time stay-at-home mother, I was ready for a new challenge. I needed and wanted to make money. I began looking for a job.

Applying for positions online was fruitless. Most of my resumes were lost in digital black holes.

I tried employment and staffing agencies. Most interviewers thought I was "too senior," "too long out of the workforce," or both to hire. It was a harsh reality. All the software had changed. I used to be adept at Microsoft Excel, but the latest version baffled me. Everything had been rearranged, relabeled, and redesigned. I hadn't a clue of how it worked. I took Excel and other computer courses at the New York Public Library to hone my skills.

One recruiter said, "You list a senior executive administrative assistant as a suitable position, but I don't think you could take orders from someone. You were the boss for many years." This comment surprised me. How did she know that? It was absolutely not true. I explained to her that my situation had changed, I really wanted to work for a CEO or president at a great company, and I believed I had the skills and experience for such a position. Whatever I said, her mind was made up.

I applied for a junior back-office position at a retailer through another employment agency. I read the job description, and knew I could manage it. And I really respected the retailer. During the second interview, the interviewer asked me to explain my previous jobs again. When I was done, he said, "You worked in advertising creating campaigns. This position is not like that. This is very tedious, unglamorous work. Are you sure you want to do this?" I said yes and explained why. I didn't get the job.

Then one day I spotted a job posting for a two-month project requiring Japanese-language skills, which I have, at a leading fashion-and-beauty media company in Manhattan. Unlike all the other job postings, this one was not linked to an online resume form. I was familiar with the company. I researched it and submitted a tailored resume and cover letter. Two days later I received an email response from a top executive with an interview invitation. I googled the executive, and thought we had a mutual passion for health and wellness, and I would really enjoy working with someone like her. I responded with a brief enthusiastic email.

As soon as I walked into her office, we hit it off. She was brilliant, enthusiastic, and filled with energy and confidence. I took her through my bilingual and bicultural professional background, which I thought more than satisfied the job description. I was honest with her about how long I'd been away from the corporate world, and I told her how much I thought I could help her on a part-time basis. She hired me. It turned out so well that two months turned into a year, and then I was asked to become a full-time employee. Today, over three years later, I'm still working for the same company—remotely—and I love working there.

Strengthened by the inspiration and confidence I gained from my adopted Nordic "sisters" back in the forests of Finland, I found the power within me to open up a new chapter in my life.

In the United States, our family maintained our Finnish connection by signing up our son for language and culture classes at the Finnish School of New York—yes, there actually is one, catering mainly to children with at least one Finnish parent—and attending cultural events staged by the Finnish consulate and the small but energetic and proud Finnish community. For the Finlandia Foundation's 100th anniversary of Finnish independence celebration in 2017, I helped bake over eight hundred Karelian pies in the basement kitchen of the Finnish church on Christopher Street in Manhattan's West Village. The pastries flew out of a pop-up café in no time and sold out before noon.

At the Independence Day reception at the Finnish ambassador's residence overlooking Central Park, I met Anna, a tall, radiant woman who stood out in traditional Karelian dress and bright red lipstick. We bonded over our mutual connections to her home country. Her maternal grandfather was born in Karelia, but he and his family had to flee during the World War II and could never return, since much of Karelia had been lost to the Soviet Union. This was a story I had heard from several people I met in Joensuu.

Though her family never talked about the war, nor was Karelian heritage present in her childhood home, Anna told me, "I have an intuitive fascination with the Karelian culture, music, food, and aesthetics. I collect traditional Karelian folk dresses and love singing Karelian songs," which is her way of paying homage to her roots and culture. As is the case with many Finnish couples, both of Anna's parents had careers—her mother as an actress, her father as an organic farmer. At times when her mother's work was thriving, her father was the main caregiver for their children while he also tended the farm. Growing up in this environment provided her the knowledge of how parents can divide and share responsibilities in an equal partnership.

I asked Anna what gender equality meant to her, as someone who has lived and worked in both the United States and Finland as an executive with the Marimekko fashion company. She explained that "the ethos of equality is culturally imbedded in the whole society of Finland. This happens in fundamental social services like health care and high-quality education, which are offered to all citizens as an essential, nonnegotiable foundation for gender equity in a society." She explained that not having college tuition debt freed her from having financial stress, enabling her to choose a career based upon her dreams, and not financial necessities.

Following Anna's logic, I realized that in order to promote equality in all aspects of the culture—gender, racial, cultural, age, and ethnic—a society needs to provide every citizen with basic tools and services that foster their well-being from birth to death, and all phases in between.

Anna acknowledged that Finland has not been completely equal, and there is much work yet to do. But she saw bright prospects for the nation to advance toward an increasingly gender-equal society. "Finland is a small country, so we must be pragmatic," she said. "We need all people to participate in democracy."

As time went on, I found myself appreciating New York City more and more—at the same time I missed Finland.

I knew I had to return to the nature and the sisterhood of Finnish Karelia, and feed my soul.

I had to go back to the Enchanted Forest.

Gateway to a
Past and Future

"I'M SORRY, BUT YOU CAN'T board the plane."

I stood at the check-in counter of a major American airline at the desolate John F. Kennedy International Airport in New York, with my husband and now-twelve-year-old son, ten giant suitcases, and boarding passes for a confirmed flight to Helsinki via London.

It was late July 2020, three years after we last left Finland. We had spent the summer months in 2016 and 2017 there, and now we were finally going back again. Or so we thought.

The COVID-19 crisis had shut down most international travel, but we had approval from the Finnish government to return to Finland as writers and researchers. My husband and I continued life as laptop-based remote workers, so we could work from pretty much anywhere in the world. We had lived through the terrible first five months of the pandemic in the middle of New York City, as tens of thousands of our neighbors died and the entire city shut down in a pre-apocalyptic collapse of sadness, fear, and suspended animation. We were very lucky and grateful that we had good health as well as continuing jobs and projects, and that the virus had not affected anyone in our immediate families or circle of friends. We also seemed to have another place to go to, a place where the virus was having very little impact.

As we entered the airline terminal, all seemed in order, and we made sure to bring along an official communication from the Finnish Border Guard confirming that we were welcome to proceed to Helsinki Airport. We had an apartment lined up in the Finnish capital.

But now we were being told by the US airline ticket counter staff that in order to board the plane to London's Heathrow Airport for our connecting Finnair flight to Helsinki, we must produce diplomatic-grade documents from the Finnish government that guaranteed our entry. Not only did the documents have to be paper originals, they had to be stamped with a fancy raised diplomatic seal. This was a brand-new, arbitrary requirement that seemed invented on the spot, a requirement that appeared in no public notice. It was also a nonstarter, since the Finnish consulate in New York told us by phone that they were not in the business of issuing such "sealed-guarantee" documents. Even if they were, we had no time to get them—our flight was leaving in three hours.

We pleaded and cajoled, but to no avail. We were stranded, sitting on our suitcases on the linoleum floor of JFK Airport, a few yards from the security gate, and we weren't flying anytime soon. We had nowhere else to go to, either, since the lease on our Manhattan apartment expired months ago, just when the virus hit New York City, and since then we were living as remotely working digital nomads with no fixed address other than short-term apartments and hotels.

We had to find a hotel until we could figure out what to do next.

I typed "hotels near me" into my smartphone. The TWA Hotel at Terminal 5 popped up. "TWA?" I asked William. I vaguely remembered press coverage of the hotel the previous year, and William remembered going there years ago to see his grandfather when he flew in from Chicago. "Is that a hotel from 1960s?" I asked. Another finger tap on the smartphone revealed startlingly beautiful images of the hotel, and it looked like nothing I'd ever seen. There was a quote from *Time* magazine that called it "the coolest hotel in New York City." Plus, they were offering rooms at a discount.

William stared wide-eyed at the pictures. "That's it! The TWA Terminal—*it's actually still there*? As a hotel? Book us a room!" We schlepped our bags to the TWA Hotel, and we stepped into a gleaming, spellbinding vision created by a Finnish-American master architect named Eero Saarinen.

A light blue vintage Volkswagen Beetle van was parked in the front parking lot, and by the main entrance a *Mad Men*–era black Lincoln Continental convertible was parked as if someone had just arrived to check in. A white awning swerved and curved above us. We stepped inside. The building's jaw-dropping architecture was an uber-glamorous, movie-set time-travel machine that instantly transported us to 1962, the year the original terminal was opened to the public.

The building also brought us forward in time, to a possible distant future when all public spaces would be designed with such spectacular beauty, and it served as a hallucinatory gateway to the possibility, however improbable at the moment, that we might somehow make it back to Finland.

This was the *Mona Lisa*, the Sistine Chapel ceiling, and the Fallingwater of the world's airport terminals, a structure that has been referred to by critics and architects as the "Grand Central of the Jet Age," "the most dynamically modeled space of its era," the "most original interior in decades," and "the sexiest building on the planet." In the words of the Yale University art professor Vincent Scully, the TWA structure is designed to "sweep us up and forward and into space," and everything about it says, "you can do it; it is going to be wonderful up there."

For nearly three weeks, as we continued to remote-work to our regular jobs in New York City and tried to see if we could plot a new route to Finland, we lived in an airport terminal, and we could almost hear Eero Saarinen's voice whispering, *You can do it; it is going to be wonderful!*

Our new temporary home was a hyper-futuristic, extraterrestrial architectural masterpiece, a thin-shelled, white-winged concrete structure that resembled a bird in flight, and as one visitor explained, it "appeared to have landed in Queens from a yet-undiscovered solar system."

When TWA went out of business in 2001, the Flight Center had been abandoned. For years it lay mostly forgotten beside a busy international airport runway, a ghost structure, but it was still there, and incredibly it had not been torn down. A developer named Tyler Morse came to the rescue, painstakingly restored the mothballed building to its original glory, and turned it into a hotel that opened a year before we got there.

Two new hotel wings with a total of 512 rooms were built on the sides of the original terminal, accessible by Saarinen's original red-carpeted, white-walled, Kubrickian tube walkways that magically ascended from the main hall. A heated pool and cocktail lounge were installed on the rooftop, offering a dramatically close view of takeoffs and landings and of the distant Manhattan skyline. Now, the skeleton-staffed, largely deserted hotel was being used mainly as a stopover for the few airline crews and essential travelers who were venturing to the skies during the pandemic.

The original TWA Flight Center was commissioned in 1958 by the reclusive, eccentric billionaire and aviation pioneer Howard Hughes, who called Eero Saarinen into his office and basically said, "Build me the most beautiful building in the world for my new terminal—and money is no object." And Eero wildly over-delivered, following his mantra that "architecture is not just to fulfill man's need for shelter but also to fulfill man's belief in the nobility of his existence on earth."

Eero, who was born in 1910 in a town just west of the Finnish capital of Helsinki, was the son of architect Eliel Saarinen, widely regarded as Finland's greatest architect of the early twentieth century, whose designs included the Helsinki Central Railway Station, Joensuu City Hall, and a master plan for a new Helsinki that wound up not being built. His son Eero studied sculpture in Paris, architecture at Yale University, and design at the Cranbrook Academy of Art in Michigan, to where Eliel had moved the family in 1925. On the international stage, Eero caught up to and even surpassed his fathers' fame, with such stylistically divergent, landmark creations as Dulles International Airport, the St. Louis Gateway Arch, Bell Labs in New Jersey, the Ingalls Hockey Rink at Yale, and the Miller House in Columbus, Indiana. To scholar Peter Papademetriou, "It is as if several architects were at work within Eero Saarinen, each pushing the limits of modern architecture in a different direction."

To me, the TWA Flight Center structure represented perhaps the farthest limits of what any architect could imagine. Walking around the leaping, swooping, free-flowing curved contours of the building, I felt like I was living inside a great ballet, a symphony, or an epic movie. "Architecture must make a strong emotional impact on man," Eero later explained, adding, "once one embarks on a concept for a building, this concept has to be exaggerated and overstated and repeated in every part of its interior so that wherever you are, inside or outside, the building sings with the same message." The message of the TWA project was, according to Eero, to "express the drama and specialness and excitement of travel." He added, "As the passenger walked through the sequence of the building, we wanted him to be in a total environment where each part was the consequence of another and all belonged to the same form-world."

We checked into our room, which protruded so close to Runway 4 that you could practically touch the jets parading majestically on the tarmac, while seven layers of triple-glazed insulated floor-to-ceiling glass windows blocked all airport noise from the room. Our son, an aviation buff, was thrilled at the twenty-four-hour show unfolding just beyond his bed. The walnut-paneled room was appointed in classic pre-Jet Age designs, including a red Saarinen Womb Chair from 1946, a white Tulip table from 1957, and David Klein TWA travel posters from the 1950s and 1960s. Completing the heavily curated retro illusion was a rotary phone resting on the table.

We explored the building in a state of dizzied disorientation. The pandemic had cut air travel to an absolute minimum, so I sometimes felt like we were the only people in the dreamlike structure. I peeked at the heated rooftop pool, where you can gaze at jets landing while you swim; at a secluded, futuristic reading room appointed in Eames furniture; at rows of sparkling, ancient coin-operated public pay phones. I studied the curved, swooping walls and floors meticulously surfaced in twenty million half-inch-diameter mosaic penny tiles to match Eero's original design, and came across a hotel display of vintage flight attendant uniforms from the designers Howard Greer, Oleg Cassini, Stan Herman, Pierre Balmain, Yves Saint Laurent, Ralph Lauren, and Valentino.

I sank into a plush seat in the Sunken Lounge in the center of the structure with my laptop and mobile phone. This became my remote office.

The immense windows of the Sunken Lounge were dominated by a view of "Connie," a 1958, propeller-driven Lockheed Constellation Starliner parked right outside on the tarmac. Connie once flew for TWA, then wandered the fringes of the aviation world by flying cargo to Alaska, delivering marijuana for a Colombian drug cartel, and being abandoned in Honduras. Mercifully, it was saved from the scrap heap for a $150 salvage fee by a gracious benefactor. Today, its outside has been restored and repainted to its original TWA-branded glory, and its inside has been retrofitted as a groovy 1960s cocktail bar.

I sat facing a giant old-fashioned Split-Flap Solari board that displayed fantasy flights and imaginary departure and arrival times for long-dead airlines and forgotten destinations. Invisible speakers throughout the hotel played an endless loop of happy, peppy, vintage pop music from the 1960s: bossa nova, the Beatles, Frank Sinatra, and Connie Francis tunes, *Promises, Promises* by Dionne Warwick, and a song that quickly became my new anthem: the Fifth Dimension's *Up, Up and Away*: "We could float among the stars together, you and I, For we can fly, we can fly!"

While I was absorbed in my laptop screen, the Split Flap board above my head suddenly became alive and several rows of flaps began flipping with metallic splatters.

Startled at the sound, I looked up. There were no planes landing or departing here, but the flaps were flipping methodically with nostalgic, quick *tap-tap-tap-tap-tap-tap* sounds. These used to be the signature sights and sounds of a departure lounge, but they had almost completely vanished from the world's airports, replaced by digital displays. Solari di Udine, the company that used to manufacture the split-flap boards, didn't even make them anymore. I walked through many airports in many cities in the last three decades, but didn't pay attention when these iconic sounds disappeared. Yet here it was, an echo of the long-past golden age of jet travel.

Basking in the incredible beauty of Eero's TWA master-piece, I thought back to magnificent public designs I had encountered in Karelia, Lapland, and elsewhere in Finland by architects like Alvar Aalto and Eero Saarinen's father, Eliel. I realized that uplifting, enlightening, and transformative public spaces like these are perhaps as essential a human right for all citizens as anything else. I used to think that beautiful environments and interiors were luxury items, something not quite necessary but nice to have. But I was now convinced that aesthetically pleasing surroundings are essential for our well-being, and they nourish our souls just as a well-balanced diet fuels our bodies.

In Joensuu, for example, our son attended second grade at a university teacher-training school that was designed expressly for the comfort and well-being of children and teachers. The principal was Professor Heikki Happonen, a longtime childhood educator and architecture history expert who was also the head of Finland's national teacher-training association. Happonen designed the school in consultation with children and teachers, and the effect was as stunning as the TWA Flight Center, creating a movie-set fantasy of what a school could look like, if it was designed for children.

The school's interior, which regularly reduces foreign visitors to stunned silence or even tears, was carefully appointed in spacious hallways, soft lighting, and warm colors selected to be especially soothing to children. A young teacher from Spain was speechless after a few minutes inside the school. "It's so beautiful," she said. "In Spain, our schools feel like prisons.

But this—this is like a dream." Couches and comic book stacks were scattered in the halls to make children feel welcome, relaxed, and comfortable, with nooks and crannies for them to relax and curl up in with a buddy or a book. The teacher's lounge, like many in Finland, was spacious and functionally elegant. This one was furnished with comfortable sofas, an espresso machine, side tables adorned with flowers in an Iittala Aalto vase, and a communal table on which a mound of fresh fruits were piled on an oversized Aalto silver serving tray. The space encouraged teachers to unwind and collaborate over coffee and snacks, and teachers even had access to a nearby faculty sauna facility.

Modular library shelves stuffed with books were moved around to create temporary meeting spaces for learning. Comfortable, old-fashioned wooden desks filled the classrooms. The science room resembled a high-tech operating theater; next to it was a cozy fireplace, and across the hall was a woodshop classroom for children to learn the essentials of carpentry in the second grade.

"School should be a child's favorite place," Professor Happonen said. "Children must feel like their school is a home for them, it belongs to them. They are very clever, they feel and appreciate an atmosphere of trust. We offer them an environment where they understand, 'This is a place where I am highly respected. I feel safe and comfortable here. I am a very important person.' My job is to protect that environment for children. That's why I come to work every day."

Life inside our temporary home of the TWA Flight Center reminded me of how many Finnish public schools are showpieces of extraordinary interior and exterior design, and upon seeing them in person I often wondered, *Why shouldn't every child and every teacher have this?*

I also thought back to our very first days in Joensuu as new arrivals to Finland, when we decided to visit a municipal swimming pool we'd heard about. I'd expected to see a typically rectangular-shaped utilitarian building, but what we stepped into was like a small resort. The curvilinear structure was positioned at the edge of the forest, with giant windows that beckoned sunlight streams to pour in through the trees. There was a deep diving pool, an Olympic–size lap pool, a shallow kiddy pool, a snack bar, a Jacuzzi and saunas, a fully equipped gym, plus a tide and wave pool that at the sound of a bell every hour released a giant wave to the delight of swimmers. Public notices were written in four languages: Finnish, Swedish, English, and Russian, and later, Arabic, to accommodate Middle Eastern refugees. It seemed remarkable that so much thought and effort was put into a city pool that was open to everybody in the community.

I then recalled the Joensuu Library, also known as the North Karelia Provincial Library, located halfway between our apartment and the university where William worked and the attached school our son attended. I expected a standard library design with rectangle rooms filled with bookshelves and reading areas. But this place reminded me of the Museum of Modern Art in Manhattan. It was a bright, airy Nordic design of such beauty that when I first entered it I wondered, *Where am I?*

Completed in 1992, the building is described by the Finnish architecture information service as "an open library landscape" that's "like a miniature city with passageways and bookshelf blocks under a high-flying roof." The description continues, "Near the entrance, at an intersection of the 'interior streets,' is the public café and newspaper reading room. Access to the other reading rooms is also from the intersection. The squares are skylighted; the sloping ceilings over the shelving blocks act as reflectors. Part of the light for the reading rooms comes through the opal glass ceiling."

My favorite spot was a purple chair by a two-story high slender bay window behind the craft book section. Our son's favorite spot soon became the amphitheater-shaped children's wing, which provided an unlimited supply of comic books, children's books, and board games. The third floor was devoted entirely to music, with comfortably furnished, soundproof music rooms you can reserve with your library card and listen to records and CDs from the library's vast collection. Our son and I reserved one of the music rooms and played an electric piano, something I'd never dreamed of doing in a public library.

The library was a theme park of books. On weekends it was one of the most populated places in town. The periodical reading room was packed with locals, and toddlers and children roamed the children's section and perched with books on curved sofas. This place is a perfect manifestation of a society that strives to enlighten and uplift all of its citizens equally.

And now here I was, stuck for an unknown time in a long-forgotten airline terminal with my family. But the architecture was so uplifting that I didn't mind at all. "TWA is beginning to look marvelous," Eero Saarinen said in the spring of 1961 as he gazed at the soaring curves of his creation under construction at Idlewild Airport, now called John F. Kennedy International Airport. "If anything happened and they had to stop work right now and just leave it in this state, I think it would make a beautiful ruin, like the Baths of Caracalla." He never saw it completed. He died five months later at the age of fifty-one of complications from surgery to remove a brain tumor.

In a practical sense, Eero's TWA project was largely obsolete soon after it opened in 1962. The structure, the baggage system, and the passenger flow were designed for 1950s propeller planes, when the largest Constellation turboprop carried just 105 passengers, but it was soon dwarfed by the arrival of the Jet Age, exploding international air traffic and much bigger commercial jet aircraft like the Boeing 707, the Douglas DC-8, and the mammoth jumbo 747, which could carry as many as 660 passengers. No one, including Howard Hughes and Eero Saarinen, could have seen the changes coming on such a scale. But the TWA Flight Center lived on, under great strain, for another thirty-nine years as TWA suffered three bankruptcies and multiple hijackings, bombings, and crashes, until 2001 when the company was dissolved and the building abandoned. "To the extent that there was a golden age of flight, it was but a moment, and it has long since passed us by," wrote Eric Wills, a senior editor at *Architect* magazine. "The project trades on a perfect past that never quite was. Yet Saarinen's bird, even if it has been caged, still sings to us: conveying the hope and possibility of distant lands, the potential for far-flung adventure and for realizing a better version of ourselves."

For twenty glorious days, we lived inside Eero Saarinen's dreamworld, and walked the halls of his resurrected relic, bathed in a narcotic architectural haze of futuristic nostalgia. Was this a dream? Would we make it back to Finland? The building seemed to say yes, and I felt content and trouble-free in its sealed-off universe.

One day we got word from British Airways that they would be happy to fly us to London so we could catch a Finnair flight to Helsinki, and that our tickets and paperwork were all in order. We said farewell to TWA and the memory of Eero Saarinen.

In mid-August, we were living in Helsinki.

Return to the Golden Land of Dreams

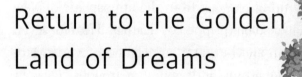

I RACED OUT OF OUR Helsinki apartment to catch the 10:19 A.M. northbound train for Joensuu.

After three years, I was going back to Karelia.

I was going to reunite with my Martha sisters.

And I was going to meet with a shaman.

Our mutual friend Irmeli told me that Helena Karhu was a brilliant anthropologist at the University of Eastern Finland, and a shamanic practitioner who knew many of the folklore and cultural traditions of Finnish Karelia. She was hosting a full moon drumming circle on an island near Joensuu, on the second full moon of October. It sounded like a perfect way to reenter Karelia and mark the progress of autumn.

The two months our family had been living in the Finnish capital seemed, like our TWA Hotel interval, to be a kind of hallucination. Until recently the weather had been crisp and pleasant; the shops, libraries, museums, and cafés were open, with pandemic-related notices. Finland was being careful, but COVID-19 was progressing at an extremely low level compared to much of the rest of the world, and the nation was functioning at about 80 percent normalcy.

It was a stunning contrast from the atmosphere of New York City, which had been gripped by death and fear for seven months. In midsummer, our familiar neighborhoods in Manhattan seemed like a rapidly decaying metropolis right out of a sci-fi movie. The city was somber and desolate, and the simple act of walking the streets left me deeply shaken by how fragile a mighty economy could be, and how swiftly the center of gravity could collapse in a magnificent, seemingly indestructible city like New York.

In the spring of 2020, when the virus began spreading globally and infections were reported in Finland, the Finnish government, under the leadership of its new, highly popular prime minister Sanna Marin, quickly declared a state of emergency, sealed the borders, suspended most international travel, encouraged office workers to work remotely from home, and soon shut down all the schools. When a virus outbreak began in the capital region, the area was sealed off with police and military roadblocks to block the spread to other areas of the country.

Since then, COVID-19 had flatlined at a very low level. Schools for seven- to fifteen-year-olds were reopened for two weeks at the end of the spring 2020 semester with very few problems, and reopened again in mid-August for the traditional start of the school year. High schools and higher education institutions remained closed throughout the pandemic.

By mid-October 2020, Finland had suffered only 351 virus-related fatalities.

So far, Finland and Norway were experiencing among the lowest per capita infection and death rates of all the European nations, and roughly 10 percent that of the United States, the United Kingdom, and of neighboring Sweden, which chose a much more laissez-faire approach to the disaster. Our seventh grade son was able to attend in-person classes every day at an English-speaking public school, which, like most Finnish public schools, was of very high quality. We felt incredibly grateful and humbled to have wound up in Helsinki during the global health crisis.

In one 2020 analysis, our new home city of Helsinki was named the best city for families out of 150 of the world's cities, and the previous year, Helsinki was ranked the world's number one city for work-life balance. It's easy to see why. The city is compact; very safe; laced with nature trails, bike and jogging paths, greenery, and good restaurants; and boasts an excellent public transportation network of trains, subways, buses, and trams.

Helsinki is a safe, ideal city for children, who often commute to school on their own as young as eight or nine years old. The city maintains a network of seventy outdoor playgrounds around the city that include free or low-cost daycare and after-school centers for children under twelve. Our son became a regular customer at Linnanmäki, a vintage amusement park that overlooks the city and is dominated by an old-fashioned wooden rollercoaster that he rode seventy-four times in a single, long late-summer day. When William asked a security guard what company owned the amusement park, the guard replied, "The children of Helsinki own it—all the proceeds go to child welfare organizations."

Fully one third of Helsinki is green area, and the city is surrounded by the *Viherkehä* (Green Ring), a network of hundreds of wooded recreational areas. "There's a green crescent around Helsinki," explained the celebrated Finnish chef Sami Tallberg, "no matter which direction you take your bike or your feet or your car, you'll come to wild nature." Tom Selänniemi, the director of Haltia, the Finnish Nature Center, explained, "You can put on a backpack in the courtyard of the Helsinki Opera House and walk along the park into the wilderness." This became one of my routine walking routes. Hesperianpuisto (Hesperian Park) located near our apartment in the Töölö district, seamlessly led to the entrance to Keskuspuisto (the Helsinki Central Park) a giant green zone of rolling, forested hills that is home to rabbits, deer, hawks, and foxes, and in many spots resembles a lush, untouched primeval forest.

In Finland, urban areas and nature are usually in the same continuum. You can move between the two spheres effortlessly or even without realizing it simply because there are no clear boundaries, and often an industrial park or a residential area sits right next to an expansive thick forest.

Soon, in winter, I would go snowshoe-walking in Helsinki's Central Park, which starts close to the city center and runs north for a well-maintained municipal park that covers 4 square miles, with a 6-mile north-south stretch. In it there are four nature reserves. Once I was off a cross-country ski or pedestrian trail, I was in the thick of a forest, stomping on fresh deep snow. I was all alone, monopolizing this precious landscape, zigzagging through and around birch, pine, and oak trees, bending under low branches and stepping over fallen trunks. As always, there was a hush, the silence that's not a complete absence of sounds. I heard birds, a half-melted stream. I loved every sensation that came with a walk in a forest. I knew that well-maintained pedestrian and bike paths cut through the park, and sometimes even highways were nearby, but I couldn't see them. I also knew many people were pushing strollers; jogging; or walking with a partner, or a dog, or all alone. This park was an integral part of the locals' everyday life. Nothing extraordinary, at least to the Finns.

Back on an off-the-beaten path, once in a while, a mountain biker zipped through the forest on a narrow groove created by other bikers and cross-country skiers. Or a couple walked a dog a few yards away, but quickly disappeared into woods. Then I was alone again. I took a screenshot of a satellite-terrain map indicating my location on my mobile phone. The image showed a thick green expanse with a single blue dot. I was in a nation's capital city—but I was in the middle of nowhere!

While Helsinki has an essential character all its own, parts of it reminded me of other great cities I'd seen in person or in photographs. The grand, ornate architecture of the tree-lined Esplanadi Boulevard dotted with chic sidewalk cafés evoked a miniature Champs-Élysées. The Senate Square at the heart of the city looks like an extension of imperial Russia—and it is, as it was built by Emperor Alexander II in 1807 when he was the head of state of the Russian Grand Duchy of Finland. A statue of Alexander II still stands in the center of the square. Helsinki's hills and trams reminded me of San Francisco and Sydney, and a waterfront promenade on the city's southern coast even resembled, in the thick of a sunny August, a little slice of the French Riviera. Helsinki's safety and cleanliness echoed that of my native Tokyo, and its surprising diversity—forty-seven international languages are taught in the Helsinki public school system—reflected that of my adopted home of New York City, though on a much smaller scale in terms of total population—Helsinki has 658,000 people, while New York City has over 8.3 million.

What is it like to live in both a cosmopolitan city and in a nature-filled environment at the very same time? At times it feels almost like a utopia, enabling one to live, work, play, thrive, and rejuvenate all at once. People are within walking distance, or just a few train or bus stops away, from art museums, concert halls, great restaurants, gourmet grocers, universities, business opportunities, medical facilities, and schools—as well as free outdoor public gyms, patches of tranquil forest and hills, tree-lined boulevards, and a coastal shore and bay dotted with sailboats, kayaks, geese, and swans.

The walk to Helsinki Central Station took me past a tucked-away statue of Larin Paraske, the nineteenth-century peasant woman who is considered the greatest of all Karelian folk singers. She carried in her mind a repertoire of hundreds of years of oral folklore and over thirty thousand *runo* songs, or sung poetic verses, including lullabies, riddles, ballads in

Kalevala meter, songs of marriage and of husbands, and *itku-virsi* crying songs, which are intense, highly emotional lamentations that help guide the souls of the departed to the hereafter.

According to one theory put forward by the contemporary Finnish violinist and composer Pekka Kuusisto, when Larin Paraske sang for Jean Sibelius in the city of Porvoo in 1891, she lit a flame of inspiration in Sibelius that transformed him into the greatest composer in Finland's history. Before the encounter, Kuusisto observed, Sibelius's music suggested he didn't have the artistic tools to achieve his destiny. But after meeting Larin Paraske, Kuusisto noted, "something clicks" in Sibelius, "and he seems to connect to a much further back time in history and the language gets suddenly transformed into something that is sort of global and eternal, something that can speak to pretty much anyone anywhere at any time." Sibelius's happy marriage and his masterpieces followed that meeting. One day I spotted a bouquet of flowers nestled in the arms of the Paraske statue, along with a mysterious, anonymous note thanking her for singing at a spot somewhere in Finland where a magnificent tree now stands over 120 years later.

My dash to the train station took me past three other masterpieces: Alvar Aalto's Finlandia Hall, a globally renowned concert and conference center; the Museum of Contemporary Art Kiasma, part of the Finnish National Gallery; and the stunning, massive, glass-and-spruce Oodi Helsinki Central Library, surely one of the world's most amazing libraries. Oodi (Finnish for "ode") was inaugurated on December 5, 2018, as Helsinki's gift to the people of Finland on the nation's one hundredth birthday, in honor of its being one of the world's most literate and library-loving nations. From its third-floor terrace, one can directly face the Parliament building eye to eye across Kansalaistori, which means "citizens' square" in Finnish. A library worker explained that the structure was built on the most valuable piece of real estate in the nation, and facing the Parliament building, so "citizens and the state are at an equal level," physically declaring the essence of democracy.

The mammoth Oodi resembles a giant boat or a whale moving through gentle waves under billowing clouds. It serves not just as a book-lending facility, but as Finland's national living room, hobby center, small business incubator complete with couches, coffee shops, a cinema and video game rooms, and as a communal work space, with free access to 3D printers, laser cutters, conference rooms, TV and music recording studios, graphic design hardware and software, and sewing machines. Everyone—from asylum seekers and homeless citizens to artists, children, students, and CEOs— are encouraged to work and relax there together, and they do. The library checks out basketballs and soccer balls, too, for those who want to play in the library's grand courtyard. Little gray self-driving, book-shelving robot wagons wheel slowly through the aisles, discreetly avoiding furniture and humans. For William and me, the flexible work and studio spaces of Oodi served as our own remote-working office space and home away from home over the last eight weeks.

By now I was familiar enough with the layout of Helsinki to take shortcuts, and I ducked around some office buildings to get to Central Station and make it onto the train to Joensuu with a few minutes to spare. Long-distance train travel in Finland is quiet, smooth, and relaxing, and I chose a single luxurious high-back swivel chair seat on the upper deck of the cafeteria car so I could enjoy the view and the good food delivered to my seat from downstairs. I parked my bags, set up my laptop and mobile phone, and settled in the last chair facing the platform. In a few minutes, announcements were made in Finnish, Swedish, and English, and the train slipped slowly out of the station. A dark mist covered the city, a familiar effect in autumn, but my spirits were high to be returning to Karelia, even for a short visit.

Not far outside of Helsinki, the scenery abruptly shifted to idyllic farmhouses, hills, lakes, and thick forest, and sunbeams sparkled through layers of clouds, spruce branches, and leaves, dancing upon lake surfaces. At one spot near the municipality of Rautjarvi, the Russian border makes an abrupt right-angle lunge westward into a lake shared by the two nations, bringing Russian waters within a few hundred feet from the train, with a Russian border guard tower visible for a few moments through the trees.

Downstairs in the train cafeteria I ordered one of my favorite Finnish dishes: hearty creamy salmon soup with potatoes, dill, and rye bread. The woman behind the counter said she'd bring it up to me—a perk of taking a seat in the dining car. In four and half hours, I was back in Joensuu. I took a short walk to my hotel through the *tori* (city center square). The city was mostly how I remembered it from 2017, with a few changes. The sidewalks were manicured with new bike and pedestrian lanes, the square was revamped with an underground parking garage and performance stage, and the park in front of the city hall and theater had been cleaned up, with some trees cut down for crime prevention.

It felt like I was home again.

The Harvest Full
Moon Drum Circle

AT 5:30 P.M., A TAXI deposited me at the edge of the tiny island of Utransaari, where I was to participate in Helena's drumming circle. I paid the driver, he squirted hand sanitizer into my cupped hand, and I received the goop with gratitude. I stepped out of the taxi and tried to figure out where to go.

The taxi driver pointed into the darkness. It was pitch black, no light of any kind except street lights behind me. Two figures jogged past and disappeared like phantoms. "Which way do I go?" I asked the driver. He gestured, "Straight that way," and then he drove away. All I could see in front of me was darkness.

I turned on my mobile phone flashlight, but it blinded me. I turned off the light and followed a narrow path with the faint light coming from the faraway streetlights. On both sides of the path was water, and I walked very slowly so I wouldn't fall into a ditch, and across a thin pedestrian bridge that connected the main land to a little island. My eyes slowly adjusting to the darkness, I stopped and turned to look toward the River Pielinen, where the dark sky, tree shadows, and shiny flat water surface merged into a serene and still beauty.

One strange, or rather, wonderful thing about being all alone in the darkness here was how incredibly safe I felt. Security was all in the air and in the water. Security was in the Finnish psyche.

When I finally stepped onto the little island after making slow steady steps and crossing the second pedestrian bridge, I stood in front of three paths. I had no clue which path to take. I had not expected this. The invitation to the drum circle included only the name of the island, with no directions or hand-drawn map. I was a bit annoyed that the organizer didn't bother to tell me how to get there. I closed my eyes and waited for a sign. I listened hard to my intuition. "I can't hear you," I begged to my intuition. I tried to summon my psychic powers.

I confidently chose the middle trail with a wooden entrance that resembled a Japanese Shinto gate, convincing myself that this had to be the one leading to the drum ceremony. I pushed on slowly, but wound up in thick bushes. My confidence evaporated. Zero psychic power. I saw no sign of a hut, and heard nothing, not a single drum, just a dark hushed forest in front of me. The trail vanished. I worried that if I went further, I'd be lost in the woods. By now, I was giving up on the drumming circle. I imagined that my host Helena's mobile phone was turned off and I couldn't reach her for directions.

This is just not meant to be, I thought. I headed back to the bridge toward the parking lot, where I'd call a taxi.

Then I saw the figure of a woman crossing the bridge and stepping onto the island, a drum under her arm. She didn't see me nor notice me, and turned to the right, walking in solitary self-absorption. I followed her along the trail a few yards behind her, silent except for our footsteps. The woman didn't seem to hear or sense me. She just kept going with the drum under her arm. *Maybe, I thought, she's a raccoon in disguise from a Japanese folktale, and she's come to rescue me.* After a while, I saw beyond her a *kota* (wooden hut) with an orange light brimming from inside. When the raccoon lady approached it, someone opened the door, a burst of orange light came out, she walked in, and the door was closed behind her. It was dark again. I walked up to the hut and opened the door. To my relief, I saw a pleasant group of people sitting around a burning fireplace, some with drums on their laps.

"Are you Naomi?" asked a tall young woman. She was Helena, the folklore scholar and shamanic teacher and practitioner. Beaming with warmth and serenity, she welcomed me in a hypnotic mezzo-soprano voice that echoed the voices of many other Finnish women I encountered. Their English skills are usually excellent, and their speech in what's typically their third language after Finnish and Swedish is sometimes slightly delayed by their attempts at precision, which seems to add an air of thoughtfulness and warm assurance to their speech. Their accent is an interesting blend of British and American flavors, influenced by English classes taught by instructors who trained in the British style, and by pop culture from the United States that many Finnish young people have grown up with, including endless reruns of shows like

Friends and *The Simpsons*. One theory for Finland's high fluency in English that much English-language TV is subtitled, because Finnish is such an obscure language that it would cost too much to dub it with Finnish actors' voices, giving Finnish children the advantage of simultaneous translation.

"Welcome to this full moon drumming circle," Helena began, alternating between Finnish and English. There were some fifteen people in the hut, and we sat in two ring circles around the fireplace. "As always, we start with spirit offerings—to the fire, to the space, and to the spirits with us today—our ancestors, nature spirits, star-beings, guardian angels, light of beings, Buddhas, bodhisattvas, yogis, yoginis, all the spirits of nature, fairies, elves, goblins, all spirits today in the circle. We evoke both energies into our beings and our silence to cultivate our lives for the fullest potential, for a long life, vitality, and well-being. It is the second full moon of this month, October. Our theme is that of abundance. It is the time of the harvest, so we can live abundantly through the wintertime until the springtime. A lot has been going in our individual and collective lives, and it's wonderful to come together to share our sounds and our silences."

Helena continued, "When we gather by the sacred fire and with offerings, it's a healing event—healing for ourselves and healing for the world. When we ask for help from the universe and from our guides and spirits, we want to offer something first. Here are three packages tied to this one piece of wood."

"The theme of this night is abundance," Helena said. "We have many people gathered here. We are thankful for the abundance of friendship in this circle tonight. It requires the openness of the heart to receive friendship and to offer friendship. I hope this spirit offering will heal our wounds from the past. We all have experiences—perhaps as children suddenly someone didn't want to play with us anymore, or someone made us question our own lovability. Those experiences unconsciously affect us. This spirit offering is about looking into our unconsciousness and inner child. How wonderful that we can do this together in this ritual way, with the sacred fire, with the help of unseen of the universe and with the help of each other."

It felt like Helena's passion and eloquence was uniting all the visible and invisible beings in and around us in the hut, on Utransaari, in the city of Joensuu, in the region of North Karelia, and all the space between us and the full moon, and beyond.

Helena passed around the three little packages tied to a piece of wood, to represent our individual and collective offerings to the spirit world. The piece of wood was from the sacred mountain of Koli, and the three packages represented the themes of abundance, the inner child, and each person's secret wish, offered collectively. One by one, we each had a moment with the offering and passed it on. When it was my turn, I held it with both hands and said prayers. The offering came back to Helena. She stood up and silently placed it on the fire. Everyone's eyes were on the offering that merged with the crackling fires.

I shifted my position on the bench so I could see the black silhouette of the offering enveloped in the bright orange fire. My face was warm. I was drenched in the intensity of the moment with all my senses. The joy, wonder, warmth, and visual sensations were sharpened after enduring so many weeks of isolation and fear earlier that spring and summer. It was surreal to be sitting with fifteen people in circles in a small wooden hut without fear during the global pandemic.

Everyone absorbed the sight of the offerings joining the fires. Helena broke the silence with a bright, "The work is well done! Now we can have fun!" She burst into spontaneous belly laughter, and we all joined in. Helena seemed to be casting a spell of love, unity, joyfulness, energy, gratitude, and anticipation of what was to come. She was letting us know that as much as this was a serious event, it was also a lighthearted, playful gathering.

She continued, "First, we start by drumming together and see what happens. Please individually tune in whatever you want to share—songs, dance, silence, words, life stories." She held her drum and a drumstick with an egg-shaped felt tip. She started drumming softly, chanting, "Have fun together, have fun drumming together, being by the fire . . ."

The drumming was abstract and nonmelodic, almost like heartbeats. I felt the vibrations on the bench, the wall, and in the air. It was a remarkable physical sensation I hadn't experienced for many years. Layers of drumming mixed with wooden sticks striking went on. I felt as if we were calling the sprits to come out and dance with us. The vibrations seemed to release pain, and invite friendship, empathy, and compassion to fill our bodies and souls. High-pitched vocals joined in, layering over the drumming sounds, then low-pitched vocals layered below the drumming. They kept mixing and projecting steady and fast beats, calling for unseen nature spirits to reveal themselves and join us for the celebration of the full harvest moon.

Slowly, the voices trailed off. The drumming slowed and stopped. Helena let out another joyful belly laugh, and it somehow seemed perfectly natural for us to join in ecstatic laughter. She invited anyone to share feelings or stories, or to simply share silence.

"Perhaps Eero will sing for us," she said.

Helena's friend Eero, an accomplished Finnish folklorist and *runo* singer, smiled and said, "Okay, I will sing 'Oravan Laulu.' It's a lullaby for the squirrels, written by the national writer Aleksis Kivi in his novel *Seven Brothers*."

In a deep, gentle voice, Eero sang:

> Makeasti oravainen.
> Makaa sammalhuoneessansa;
> Sinnepä ei Hallin hammas.
> Eikä metsämiehen ansa,
> Ehtineet milloinkaan . . .

> *Sweetly a little squirrel*
> *lies in his moss room*
> *the place that wolf's teeth*
> *or hunter's trap could never reach.*

> *From his high chamber*
> *he looks at the world*

many battles under him
but a branch of a conifer, the peace flag
fluttering above him.

Such happy living
in the swinging cradle castle
there swings the little squirrel
in the dear spruce
on the mother's chest
listening to the kantele of the forest.

There sleeps the Sway-tail
front of his little window
singing birds under the sky
walk him in the evening
to the Golden Land of Dreams.

After a pause, Helena suggested that we think of being our favorite animal spirit during the next drumming session. "Let yourself express freely—you can sing, you can howl. Don't worry. If we sense that you've gone too far, we will gently bring you back. If you choose to let the silence be your ultimate expression, that is a good option, too."

A single drum slowly began beating, then another, and another, until the hut was booming, and all the people and spirits inside it were swept into their vibrations. How long or short this went on, I do not know. It felt like forever; at the same time it was a fleeting moment. It was personal, communal, and universal. We were in an all-out trance, drumming, singing, dancing, and chanting.

After the drumming stopped, Helena invited her guests to share their animal spirit experiences. One guest said she was soaring in the sky like an eagle and saw her family down below. Another said he was dashing through the forest like a deer. Everyone told a vivid, descriptive story.

It all made sense for this full moon drum circle to take place far away from city lights and on a small island that could be reached only on foot by crossing the two bridges. A place so close yet so far. It was a pilgrimage. Every step prepared me for the fullest immersion with the ritual, nature spirits, sounds, sensations, vibrations, and last but not least, the people who gathered there.

"If you ever feel lonely in the future," concluded Helena, "you can remember this evening."

Helena promised to take me soon to one of the most sacred places in Karelia, a place that some believe is the ancestral heart and soul of Finland. I hadn't the slightest idea what the experience would be like. *I'll find out when I get there,* I thought.

I stepped out of the hut. I knew my way around this time. I traced back the trail. It was brighter outside. I looked up at the sky and saw the bright white, full moon. I savored the abundance of nature's gifts and the abundance of new encounters.

The harvest moon illuminated my path toward home.

Women in Charge

THE MOST ADMIRED WOMAN IN Finland today is Tarja Halonen.

She is a basketball-playing, cat-loving, seventy-seven-year-old lawmaker and grandmother who served as Finland's first female president, from 2000 to 2012.

On a recent winter day in Helsinki, in the same week that she was named the most admired woman in a public poll by YLE, Finland's national public broadcaster, William and I waited for President Halonen to speak with us through our computer screen, as COVID-19 precautions prevented us from meeting in person.

Despite her exalted stature, I felt relaxed for the interview, perhaps because I had seen her disarming, charming demeanor in many photos and videos.

There are many photos of President Halonen with other world leaders, but one series of images really stood out for me. As her national next-door neighbor, Russian president Vladimir Putin hosted her or came calling many times during her twelve years in power. In image after image, echoing the effect that fellow Finnish superwoman Riitta Uosukainen had on him, Putin looks at Halonen like a shy, deferential junior supplicant in the presence of a force much more powerful than himself.

President Halonen walked in and sat down in front of her computer facing us, all smiles.

I was eager to hear her reflections on the power of Finland's nature and the power of Finland's women.

I asked her what her leadership secret was.

"You don't have to be an iron lady," she said. "Iron is too hard. You should be extremely strong but flexible. And you have to have a lot of humor towards yourself."

Former president Halonen came from humble, working-class roots in the Helsinki neighborhood of Kallio, where she still lives today. Her mother was a domestic worker who grew up in an orphanage, and her father was an electrician. Halonen earned a law degree, and served as general secretary of the National Union of Finnish Students, an attorney with the Central Organization of Finnish Trade Unions, chair of the Finnish National Organization for Sexual Equality, a member of Parliament for the Social Democratic Party, and as Finland's first female minister of justice and first female minister of foreign affairs.

"Nature is a part of everything in Finland," she explained, "from school trips to nature destinations, to the very big role that summer cottages play in the lives of so many Finnish families, not just the elite." Halonen is a lifelong Helsinki resident, but like most Finnish people, she was suffused in nature from a very young age. Every summer she spent three months in the countryside with family friends, foraging and exploring the woods. "We couldn't get blueberry pie if we didn't take part in picking those blueberries," she remembered with a grin. Foraging, cooking, and eating treasures from nature is a recurring theme for Finns both rural and urban.

For Halonen, her biggest dose of nature comes in the form of a community allotment garden plot in Helsinki that she has owned for forty years. There are eight such mega gardens in Helsinki, which typically consist of scores of small cottages and lushly vegetated garden plots connected by gravel paths. They create the deep fantasy of rural green life inside a metropolis. The gardens first appeared in the early twentieth century as places for workers to escape and rejuvenate, very close to home. It was refreshing to discover a former president having a community cottage garden in the city, not a gated high-fenced mansion with professional gardeners.

Halonen explained, "If you have lived all your life in nature or near it, you almost don't notice it, you just feel it. You notice it when you are somewhere else where you cannot have it." *Yes*, I thought. I have the reverse experience. I noticed the abundance of nature everywhere in Helsinki, because I was not used to seeing it in cities I'd lived in all my life.

She continued, "My relationship with the outdoors in everyday life is very natural. In my free time I like hiking, gardening, and swimming in natural waters."

Turning to social and political affairs, I asked Halonen, "Why do women in Finland have such a relatively strong position in society?"

Halonen thinks the answer lies in history, hardship, and struggle. "Finland is a small nation," she said. "For seven hundred years we were a part of our western neighbor. Then the king of Sweden started a war against Russia and he lost it. Then we were one hundred years a part of Russia, luckily as an autonomous part. Now our independence has lasted a little more than one hundred years, we have had one civil war and two wars and many difficulties. We have learned to be very independent and stubborn and hardworking. Perhaps somehow it has been easier for us to realize that you need both men and women for a society to function at 100 percent. Here in the North we have a long tradition of strong women in society. The women have to be strong in order to survive and in order to help their families and their fellow citizens."

"In 2000 there were several female candidates running for president," Halonen recounted, "and my victory was a natural consequence of gender progress that was already under way in Finland. We didn't underline the fact that I was a woman too much in the election campaign. We Finns are used to being quiet in certain ways, so we all understand what the issue is, but we don't say it. Perhaps our history has been the key—we understand the music but also the silence." When she became president, Halonen remembered, little girls rejoiced, thinking, "Now we can all become lorry drivers or pop singers or presidents, or whatever we want!"

With a twinkle in her eyes, Halonen told of receiving a letter from a little boy who asked, "Madame President, is it true that boys cannot become president anymore?" She answered him,

"My dear, of course they can! It's possible for both the boys and the girls."

The significance of a woman being a nation's highly popular democratically elected president for six years, and then being reelected for her achievements for another six years, struck me as revolutionary. I had no frame of reference for it. The closest thing to it that I could remember was the story of Margaret Thatcher, the "Iron Lady" British prime minister from 1979 to 1990.

In my adopted country of the United States, we've never had a female president. My home country of Japan is believed to have had some eight empresses in its 1,800-year history, but the last one was in 1771. In the second century A.D., a popularly-chosen sorceress-queen named Himiko was said to have peacefully reigned over Yamatai, a predecessor state of Japan. According to the Chinese text *Records of the Three Kingdoms*, when Himiko died, a bloody period of chaos, assassination, and murder unfolded. A relative of Himiko named Iyo, a girl of thirteen, was made queen and order was restored.

I wondered what it would be like to grow up in a modern nation where men and women had equal opportunities, powers, and responsibilities in society. I wondered what it would be like to grow up in a country where a single mother from a working-class family could become president.

During our virtual meeting, former president Tarja Halonen wondered aloud, "Are female leaders different? I seriously don't know. We have not had enough cases yet to draw scientific conclusions." But she took pride in how the female-dominated Finnish government had handled the first year of the COVID-19 pandemic. "We have a coalition government of different political parties, and all five of the leaders are women," she noted. "They are very young, only one is over forty. They are all very, very capable. Especially now in the time of the pandemic I think it's made a big difference, because they have a good understanding of the crisis, like the female leaders of Norway, New Zealand, and Taiwan."

Now in her post-presidency, Tarja Halonen continues to work on the issues she is most passionate about, including human rights, worker's rights, gender equity, problems of globalization and inequality, and sustainable development.

She traces her longtime support of LGBTQI rights back to a consciousness-raising moment she had when her now-adult daughter was a little girl. Discussing one of the girl's friends, the elder Halonen remarked, "I don't know if that one is a boy or a girl." The daughter replied in a firm voice, "It is not our business, Mommy!" It was, former president Halonen explained, "A question of another child's humanity."

Today, Finland's first female president says she is happy to live in a nation where "children still have their childhood, and can play."

"If you have to face something that is unknown, like the future, you have to be creative," Halonen explained. "We can't give children a blueprint for the future, but we can try to find the basic issues and ideas which could help them create the systems they will need in the future."

She added, "I think today it's very important both in my own country and in others and in international politics that we have both men and women in power because we need a broad scope of opinions and know-how and skills."

As for Finland's future on the world stage, Halonen quipped, "If you're not too crazy, you realize you can't change the world alone."

"But you can be an encouraging example. You can show the world that it is possible."

———————

ON DECEMBER 12, 2019, the assembled leaders of Europe stood in the lobby of a sleek office building in Brussels and waited.

They were waiting for a highly charismatic young Finnish woman to arrive and take charge.

Her name was Sanna Marin. She was the world's youngest national leader, a thirty-four-year-old mother who was raised in a low-income, LGBTQI family, who two days earlier was elected to become the prime minister of Finland as the leader of a five-party coalition headed by five women, four of them under the age of thirty-five.

Marin was coming to preside over a summit meeting of the European Council, the leadership body of the European Union, and the officials included German chancellor Angela Merkel, French president Emmanuel Macron, and the heads of twenty-four other European nations, from Norway and Denmark to Slovenia and Cyprus. Finland was acting in the rotating role of presidency of the European Council, which made Marin the presiding host of the event.

The leaders were lining up for a group photo, but Marin was nowhere to be seen.

Finally, with perfect celebrity timing in a flurry of photographer's shutter clicks, Marin arrived last, and was beckoned by the president of the European Union to take the front-and-center position of the photo opportunity, surrounded by her fellow heads of government. This was Sanna Marin's debut on the world stage, and her delighted expression reflected the astonishing journey that took her to this moment.

Marin's parents separated when she was a toddler, and she was raised near Helsinki by her highly supportive mother and her mother's female partner. Even then, in the 1990s, same-sex relationships were not legally recognized and rarely talked about in Finland, and Marin later said she felt invisible because she couldn't talk about it. "The silence was the hardest," she explained. "Invisibility caused a feeling of incompetence. We were not recognized as a true family or equal with others. But I wasn't much bullied. Even when I was little, I was very candid and stubborn."

In the years since, Marin has seen her father, who she explained had an alcohol problem, only once. Her own mother grew up in an orphanage, and Marin's childhood unfolded in conditions of what she described as an "abundance" of love but constant money pressures. "Like many other Finns," she once confided, "my family is full of sad stories."

Marin explained, "For me, human rights and equality of people have never been questions of opinion but the basis of my moral conception." She added, "I joined politics because I want to influence how society sees its citizens and their rights." Marin was the first person in her family to attend university, worked as a baker and cashier, earned a master's degree, and quickly moved up the ranks of the center-left Social Democratic Party. At twenty-seven she was elected to the Tampere City Council, and was elected as a member of Parliament in 2015. Marin won viral attention in Finland with YouTube clips of her as the no-nonsense vice chair of the Tampere City Council, calmly and forcefully running meetings and scolding long-winded speakers.

When I first saw the media coverage of Marin, I was impressed by how she reminded me of many Finnish women I had met. Her youth and star-power were already igniting a global media frenzy, and she projected the image of an archetypal modern Finnish woman—highly educated, confident, strong, multilingually articulate, and deeply versed in social and world affairs.

In 2018, Marin was appointed as the nation's minister for transport and communication, and she became prime minister on December 10, 2019. Her ascension as Finland's head of government struck the nation like a burst of fresh air, and local headlines proclaimed "Feminism Comes of Age in Finland" and "Women Rule: What We've Been Waiting For." Her personality astonished domestic and foreign audiences, who had grown accustomed to an older, male-dominated Finnish government that was in power from 2015 to 2019. Finland had two female prime ministers before, but the first, Anneli Jäätteenmäki, served for barely two months in 2003, while the second, Mari Kiviniemi, served for a year in 2010–2011 before resigning in the wake of low public support for her party.

Sanna Marin, on the other hand, was "a one-in-a-generation natural political talent," according to former

Finnish prime minister Paavo Lipponen. One reporter enthused, "Her performance at press conferences and in Parliament has been just what works best for Finns, clear, concise, unemotional; but with an undertone of warmth." Helsinki University researcher Timo Miettinen stated, "People have been saying it's the best thing to happen to the international reputation of Finland." Marin joined in the excitement, writing, "I'm extremely proud of Finland. Here a poor family's child can educate themselves and achieve their goals in life. A cashier can become even a prime minister."

On the day Marin took power, in the municipality of Ilomantsi on the Russian border, a sixty-five-year-old man named Veikko reported that he was "very happy that we now have a young female PM with fresh new thoughts on how to lead our beautiful country. She is well educated, bright, and does not take any BS from anybody. She is a strong independent woman and a bright new star for her generation. I'm sure she will make a good example for all the young men and women of our world."

A student named Ella in Helsinki went further, confessing, "I cannot recall when politics last made me cry tears of happiness. This did. I experienced my political awakening at age sixteen. The power that rose from the 2015 elections four years earlier didn't look like me. This, now, is what politics is supposed to look like. It is supposed to look into the future, think of the welfare of the people." To younger Finnish people, "of course she is a role model," said twenty-six-year-old graduate student Vuokko Schoultz. "Look at where she came from," she noted of Prime Minister Marin's working-class background. "I think she is the best prime minister we have had in many years."

Marin is a leader of the Instagram generation—during her swift rise to power she chronicled her life on her Instagram page, including photos of her regular attendance at Pride events. In the international media, the adulation for the prime minister sometimes veered toward the extreme. An April 2020 *Vogue* magazine feature story gushed that "Marin has smooth, pale skin, round cheeks highlighted with a tiny bit of pink rouge, and alert green-blue eyes. When she speaks, she comes across as measured and a bit remote, quite cautious, but also warm. Here in Finland, where people tend to speak their minds directly or keep their counsel, she has a quiet dynamism, exuding composure and competence. She's less a firecracker than an eco-sustainable light bulb: slightly low-wattage and a bit cool, but trusted, dependable, and likely to last a long time." When she became prime minister, *Vogue* explained, "Finnish politics, often overlooked—coalitions are seldom glamorous—suddenly seemed rare and exciting." The article speculated "she is, perhaps, the only PM who posts breastfeeding selfies on Instagram, or pasta sauce recipes on Facebook."

Marin also proved to be a master of media quotes. At a meeting of the World Economic Forum in Davos, Switzerland, in January 2020, she said, "I feel that the American Dream can be achieved best in the Nordic countries, where every child, no matter their background or the background of their families, can become anything, because we have a very good education system." She added, "We have a good health care and social welfare system that allows anybody to become anything. This is probably one of the reasons why Finland gets ranked the happiest country in the world."

As Finland effectively managed the COVID-19 pandemic through 2020, Marin and her female-dominated government coalition were praised by some observers as exemplars of superior leadership by women, along with the female heads of countries like New Zealand, Iceland, and Norway, which were experiencing relatively low COVID-19 rates. As the *South China Morning Post* put it in June 2020, "These countries are among those with the lowest numbers of cases, deaths and, so far, the best responses to the coronavirus crisis. They also share a striking similarity: they are run and governed by strong, decisive and empowered female leaders." Marin, however, was skeptical. "There are countries led by men that have also done well," she told the BBC. "So I don't think it's a gender-based issue. I think we should be more focused on what the countries that have done well have learned."

This was typical of Marin's brushing aside the media buzz about her looks, her youth, and her gender. "Maybe it's not as big a deal in Finland as it would be somewhere else," she told *Time* magazine, and after all, nearly half of Finland's members of Parliament were female by 2020, and she was the nation's third female prime minister. "In every position I've ever been in, my gender has always been the starting point—that I am a young woman," she said, "I hope one day it won't be an issue, that this question won't be asked. I want to do as good a job as possible. I'm no better and no worse than a middle-aged man." When she took power, she explained it wasn't "that big a deal" for women to be in power. "Hopefully in the future it will be the new normal," she stated, adding, "I have concentrated on the fact that we have a lot of work to do."

Marin's personality was a vivid, complementary counterpoint to that of Finland's president since 2012, the seventy-two-year-old Sauli Niinistö, a rollerblader, former judge and police chief, former justice and finance minister, and strong advocate for gender progress himself. Niinistö was no stranger to adversity either, having lost his first wife of twenty years in a fatal road accident, and surviving death in Thailand during the 2004 Indian Ocean earthquake and tsunami by climbing a utility pole with his son.

In 2009, Niinistö married Jenni Haukio, a journalist twenty-nine years his junior, with whom he now has a three-year-old son. In the Finnish system, the president focuses on foreign, military, and ceremonial affairs as the head of state, while the prime minister focuses on day-to-day domestic government operations. In late 2020, the public approval levels of both Sanna Marin and Sauli Niinistö were so consistently high that *Foreign Affairs* magazine wrote that "Finland arguably has the most popular democratically elected government in Europe," adding that Niinistö was "the only Western leader who could be said to have good relations with both Russian President Vladimir Putin and U.S. President Donald Trump."

When our family was living in Helsinki as new arrivals, Prime Minister Marin triggered Instagram moments that enlarged her celebrity status to even higher orders of magnitude. The first surprise came in August 2020, when Marin announced her recent marriage to Markus Räikkönen, a business executive and her longtime partner since they were both eighteen. She posted wedding photos of their small outdoor ceremony at Kesäranta, the ornate, nineteenth-century wooden villa on the banks of the Baltic Sea that has been the official residence of Finnish prime ministers since 1919. "Sanna Marin looked spectacular in a floor-length off-white ethereal gown with long sleeves and a flowing veil pinned in her hair," *Tatler* magazine reported breathlessly. "Her bouquet was made up of cream peonies and foliage, while her groom—a former Finnish association football player—looked smart in a classic tuxedo."

In announcing the wedding, Marin posted on Instagram, "Yesterday we said to each other I will. I am happy and grateful that I get to share my life with the man I love. We have seen and experienced a lot together, shared joys and sorrows, and supported each other at the bottom and in the storm. We have lived together in our youth, grown up and grown older to our beloved daughter. Of all the people, you're right for me. Thank you for being by my side."

Before becoming prime minister, Marin had split her six months parental leave in half with her husband, so each could spend time with their now-three-year-old daughter. Once in power, Marin and her government announced plans to expand and equalize parental leave to both parents in a family, granting almost seven months of paid leave to each parent, for a total of fourteen months per couple.

In October 2020, a photo appeared in the Finnish fashion magazine *Trendi* of Marin wearing a stylish black blazer with a plunging neckline, and apparently no blouse or shirt underneath it. The striking image triggered an uproar of controversy between critics who condemned the outfit as inappropriate for a prime minister, and supporters who defended her right to circulate a glamorous picture of herself. In her defense, hundreds of Marin's supporters, both female and male, flocked to Twitter to post pictures of themselves in similar outfits and poses, using the hashtag #ImWithSanna.

For most of her term in office, however, Marin stayed laser-focused on the critical aspects of her job. "Finland is not a dream world," she said. "We also have problems." She explained, "We all have to fight each and every day for equality, for a better life," adding "it's not somebody else's job."

In her first prime minister's New Year message, Marin wrote that she wants Finland to be a "financially responsible, socially equitable and environmentally sustainable society." Her goals include making progress on the gender pay gap, making the country carbon-neutral by 2035, reducing domestic violence, strengthening the education system, and reforming the country's antiquated laws on rape and transsexuality.

"I want to build a society where every child can become anything and every person can live and grow in dignity," Marin once said. "The strength of a society is measured not by the wealth of its most affluent members, but by how well its most vulnerable citizens are able to cope. The question we need to ask is whether everyone has the chance to lead a life of dignity."

In a speech delivered in March 2021, Marin noted, "Women's full and equal participation in society has made Finland's development possible. A hundred years ago, Finland was a poor and conflict-torn society. It was not possible for us to ignore the potential of half of our population."

Like many other world leaders, the issue Marin is most likely to be judged on is how she and her officials manage the COVID-19 pandemic. In mid-March 2020, she took unprecedented action by locking down much of the nation and invoking the Emergency Powers Act, which appeared to tame the virus to extremely low levels for the rest of the year. Exactly a year later, when a spike in infections broke out, Marin took similar decisive actions and led the nation into a second widespread shutdown, which appeared to be successful and was eased in June 2021.

In July 2021, the German news magazine *Der Spiegel* ranked Finland as the most successful nation in the world in dealing with the COVID–19 crisis. The index was based on four criteria: excess mortality, restrictions on people's lives and freedoms, GDP performance compared to pre-pandemic projections, and first-dose vaccination coverage.

If Marin succeeds in leading the country out of the crisis, her future may be a very bright one—a recent poll ranks her as the nation's number one choice to succeed President Sauli Niinistö when his second and final term expires in 2024.

Goddess of Fog and Mists

There are many other legends,
Incantations that were taught me,
That I found along the wayside,
Gathered in the fragrant copses,
Blown me from the forest branches,
Culled among the plumes of pine-trees,
Scented from the vines and flowers,
Whispered to me as I followed
Flocks in land of honeyed meadows,
Over hillocks green and golden . . .

—THE *KALEVALA*

I SAT ON A CLIFF and communed with the spirits of Finland.

Thick shrouds of fog crept up the sides of Koli, the 1,138-foot hill that dominates the region's flatlands and forms the spiritual heart of Karelia, and the nation. The mist obscured the normally majestic view of Lake Pielinen and the endless forests that stretch out to every horizon.

Beside me was Helena, the anthropologist and shaman who'd led the full moon drum circle in Joensuu. Coming up the hill behind us were my husband and son, and Helena's friend Eero, the singer of Finnish and Karelian hymns and poetry, or *runo*. "Some *runo* make you cry, and some make you strong," Eero noted.

Helena had offered to take us here for a day of reflection and renewal, at a place of great spiritual importance to her and many other Finns and visitors. This was a favorite place of awe and inspiration for Finnish artists, writers, and composers ever since the golden age of the 1890s, when a feeling of romantic nationalism called Karelianism blossomed and helped give birth to the nation's independence. I had been to the summit of Koli a few times before, and had admired the expansive view of Lake Pielinen below steep cliffs rich with spruce and birch forests.

"This is such a majestic place," I marveled.

Helena replied, "This is a place of healing and strength and guidance. I believe that periods of contemplation and meditation are our foundation for mental stability. In the Finnish tradition we haven't had the meditation or contemplation practice in the same way as in Japan, India, or China, but our way of living has been very meditative. If you pick blueberries, or forage mushrooms, or go ice fishing, they are so meditative. Finns are silent. We are comfortable with the silence of nature. And the silence of the mind."

According to Finnish folklore, these lands were teeming with trolls, elves, spirits, and demons. Chief among them was Tapio and his wife, Mielikki, the god and goddess of the forest. Tapio was tall and slender, wore a peaked hat of leaves and a coat of moss, and Mielikki was bedecked in fine jewels and pearls. They lived in a grand wooden castle somewhere in the forest, and hunters prayed to them in the hope of a successful hunt. The *Maahiset* were tiny, irritable trolls who lived under trees and houses, and the *Kirkonväki*, or church folk, were little creatures who lived under church altars and eased the sorrow of suffering worshipers.

Today, the spirit most in evidence seemed to be Untar, the female deity who lived in the highest regions of the heavens and governed the fogs and mists, which she passed through a silver sieve before sending them down to earth. Helena had been coming here to Koli National Park for over forty years, since she was an infant, and never before saw so a thick a fog as now. "The climate is inviting us to look inward" by blocking our views, she speculated. A gentle wind arrived.

The smooth granite dome we sat on was called Akka-Koli (Old Woman Koli), the companion to Ukko-Koli (Old Man Koli) a nearby slightly higher peak. In Finnish mythology, Ukko is the oldest and most powerful of all the gods and spirits, controlling thunder, harvests, strength, and prosperity, and his wife and close partner, Akka, is described as a mighty goddess. This giant gray quartzite hillock was a last vestige of a volcanic mountain archipelago that soared over the continent about 1.9 billion years ago. The rock curved away to a treacherous, unseen drop-off.

"I am 100 percent Karelian from my roots," said Helena. "My mother's family is from Liperi, which is at the very core of North Karelia. On my father's side, I am a sixth-generation Karhu from Joensuu. Before that, the Karhus came from Viipuri, which is now Vyborg, in Russian Karelia." She explained how Karhu means "bear," the generally shy forest creatures who were worshipped as divine and intelligent spirits by tribal cults in Finland, and nicknamed "Honey Paw of the Mountains," "Pride of the Thicket," and "The Fur-Robed Forest Friend."

When Helena was a little girl, she went to visit her elderly maternal grandmother, whom she was very close to, only to discover that the woman had suffered a stroke and could no longer speak. Helena remembered, "I found these words on a paper on her table when my mother and I found her: *You have the strength and wisdom of the ancient pines, and the lightness and flexibility of the blades of grass.*" The words were her last message to her daughter and granddaughter.

On the summit of Akka-Koli the wind and fog intensified, reducing visibility to just a few yards. William hunkered down low on the slippery cliff on his hands and knees to avoid being blown off to oblivion.

Atop the summit, unperturbed, Helena and Eero reached into their sacks, and pulled out drums and drumsticks. Helena closed her eyes and intoned, "I'd like to call out to our ancestors, guardian angels, enlightened beings, Buddhas, bodhisattvas, yogis, fairies, elves, and nature spirits to be present for us here today, and offer us guidance. Our minds are at ease as we enter the meditative state of no thoughts, nothing to do, nowhere to go. We feel this white rock quartz under our feet, and we connect to this ancient strength."

Eero started to drum gently and faintly. Helena joined in. Eero said, "We are going to sing a song dedicated to Mother Earth. Different trees like birch, aspen, alder, and pine are growing from different parts of the earth. Mother Earth is carrying all of us. I sing and you respond." Eero sang a beautiful Karelian folk tune, and we repeated his verses. This went on for a while as the drumming got louder and mingled with the wind.

A now-fierce wind whipped around us. With my eyes closed, I perched on the rock and listened to the drumbeats, wind, and leaves and branches swinging and dancing.

I wasn't sure if our son would want to come with us on this pilgrimage, but he joined in enthusiastically, and now he was sprawled on his belly on the side of the peak, jamming with a drum.

The drumming slowed. Wind gushed all around us. Helena leaned down and rested her forehead on the rock surface. I too put my head down on the rock, and I absorbed lingering vibrations in all my body. I tuned into everything around me, and reconnected with the whole wide universe. In a year of global tragedy, pain, and fear, and after nearly thirteen years of the joys and challenges of motherhood, this was a powerful feeling of healing and renewal for my body and soul. I looked inward, as nature was urging me to. I thought of how this moment was a kind of spiritual synthesis for our family, connecting multiple strands of belief together with sound and nature.

When our son was born, like most parents, I felt this tiny creature was the most beautiful thing I had ever seen. William and I held an interfaith family "spiritual welcoming" service for him at the Church Center of the United Nations in New York, in a chapel that displayed symbols from all the world's major faiths. Growing up in Japan, I learned morals in a culture that was intertwined in daily custom with Buddhism, Taoism, and Confucianism, and I attended a Catholic middle and high school, where Jesus and Mary were symbols of universal love. Living in New York City, I became familiar with other faiths. Passages from one reading at our child's service echoed in my memory, from the Native American "Prayers Presenting an Infant to the Sun" and "Introducing a Baby to the Cosmos": "Today we are blessed with this beautiful baby.... May he walk and dwell on Mother Earth peacefully.... All is peaceful, all in beauty, all in happiness. Now this is the day our child is blessed into the daylight.... When your road is fulfilled in your thoughts may we live, may we be the ones whom your thoughts will embrace."

Nearly thirteen years had passed since that ceremony. Having a child is one of the most rewarding and challenging responsibilities a person can have. There is no practice run or operations manual; every child is unique. It is hard work, filled with unknowns, doubts, and mistakes. It is full-time, physical, emotional, psychological, spiritual, and cosmic all at once. It tests your stamina, instinct, intelligence, and patience. To me, the most priceless by-products of raising a child are to see the world through the child's eyes, and to grow in ways you never knew possible. I strive to be a role model, because children learn from watching parents more than listening to them. Sometimes my husband and I fail, and sometimes we succeed. I try to reexamine my behaviors and try to improve them as much as possible. Perhaps we have children not to raise them but to be enlightened by them.

I hoped our son would remember this moment in the wind with his parents and friends drumming on top of a mountain.

I hoped he would remember what it was like to be a child in New York City, where so much of what was creative and noble and challenging in the world came together, and what it was like to be a child in Finland, where children were allowed to be children and encouraged to live and learn not through stress and overwork but through movement, discovery, laughter, and play.

I hoped he would remember the privilege of living in a society where people cared for one another as deeply as they do here, and a society that honored women and girls as highly as they do here.

Eero and our son retreated to the visitor's center to dry off over a hot lunch, while Helena beckoned William and me to go deeper with her into Koli's nature.

"There is a cave I'd like to show you," she said. "It is a place where few people go, as it's difficult to find and to reach. It has no name, and most people don't know about it. It is one of the most sacred sites around here. Usually a sacred place is not an easy place to access. It has to be little difficult to get to."

She took us down a steep slope with no trail, just rough vegetation, branches, and mud that we slipped and slid down on. Shrouds of thick fog lingered, creating an eerie, cinematic fairyscape that cloaked the perilous drop-offs nearby.

We crept along the side of the mountain and came to a huge protruding triangle-shaped rock complex, a few feet from a sheer cliff. It looked like the profile of a bear head. Helena ducked, went under its jaw, and disappeared to the other side. We followed. I saw a slanted triangle opening behind the giant bear head rock. Helena bent down and walked into it. I followed. We were now in a cocoon. It was quiet. There was no wind. We were sitting behind the bear's head. Helena sat down at the deepest end of the cave and started to take some items out of her backpack.

"We are now in the womb of Mother Earth," she said. "We're in the womb with our ancestors. And we are in the realm of fairies."

"I have a gift for you," Helena said. "I made this at home, and it felt to me like an invitation for you to enter this world of Koli." She handed me a shoulder-width narrow object wrapped in a beige cloth. I unwrapped it and found a slender, elegant drumstick with a felted tip of pastel pink, light gray, dark blue, and black.

I asked, "Did you make the felt tip, too?"

Helena said, "Yes, I made the whole thing. The black and gray are from natural Finnish lamb's wool, the pink and blue is Nepalese felt, and the handle is pine from North Karelia." I loved it.

She took out a candle. "It is from Eero," she said, "He brought them back from the Valamo Orthodox Monastery. I will make a fire for you."

Helena turned to a small enclosed space in the cave formed by boulders. She lit the candle and let it stand between small rocks. The light shot straight up, and a warm orange glow spread from its center. Helena spoke of the energies of nature and consciousness and offered prayers and blessings for the growth and happiness of our family.

The cave became a shrine inside Koli, the heart and soul of Finland. In this makeshift forest temple, which felt as authentic to me as any ornate church, temple, or shrine, surrounded by ancestors and nature spirits, I prayed for strength and wisdom to help me face the challenges of life. Helena began to shake a maraca. My eyes were open, but I saw nothing. My ears were open, but I heard nothing. My mind was opening up in this sacred rock cave brimming with the orange glow.

———————

"THERE IS ONE more place I want to show you," Helena said. "The Tarhapuro waterfall. It is connected to the fairy realm, to the world of nature spirits. They help us step into realms of childhood within us and remind us to be innocent and playful. I've learned much from them." We drove to a parking spot beside Lake Pielinen and Helena, William, and I entered the forest and a peaceful, herb-rich green valley.

Helena and I became separated from William and hiked up a boulder-strewn hillside toward the rushing, idyllic waterfall. Helena said quizzically, "I don't feel the presence of fairies here today. They are not here."

On the hike back to the road, we ran into William, who was very excited about something.

"I saw them!" he exclaimed. "I really saw them!"

"What," I asked, "fairies?"

"No, their houses—they're everywhere!" I wondered what he'd been smoking out there in the woods.

Later, William showed me pictures he'd taken of a scene he couldn't believe. Somewhere on the side of the mountain he had come across a vast complex of doorway-shaped tiny holes in the slope that resembled Hobbit-like entranceways. Many of them had terrace-like patches of ground in front of them, abstract-colored designs over them, and strangest of all, micro-evergreen trees planted on either side of the "doorways." He reported seeing scores of them, and he figured the fairies were inside sleeping, or maybe off to a convention somewhere else. It all seemed pretty real at the time, and the pictures seemed to back up his story. We'll have to go back there some day and investigate further.

Our last stop of the day was a beach on the shore of Lake Pielinen, where Eero serenaded us with a farewell Karelian *runo* song.

As a parting thought, Helena offered us her speculation on what was most special about this place. "Some researchers believe that this Karelian region is the land of the woman," she said. "There was traditionally a very matriarchal way of living here in the pre-Christian era. I feel like the energy of people of North, the Nordics, is largely female. The North is the realm of the spirit, and in the realm of the spirit, everything is equal, and there is a humble respect by each gender for the other, where you don't place yourself first, then there is true support for everyone in society."

"Maybe that's where our spirit of equality came from," Helena said. "Maybe we can help bring such balance to the rest of the world."

The Land of Women

IN DISTANT MYTH AND MEMORY, there are scattered clues that point to a "Land of Women" that once existed in present-day Finland.

According to the Finnish literary scholar Kaarina Kailo, the idea of Terra Feminarum, a mysterious northern Land of Women, "has intrigued scholars for centuries," as far back as the Roman historian Tacitus in 98 A.D., and Adam von Bremen, a German medieval chronicler who wrote of Terra Feminarum as a land east of Sweden that was run by women.

In Adam von Bremen's account, written in 1075 A.D., he described Terra Feminarum as a land of fierce, nature-worshipping Amazons who dwelled between Sweden and the Russian border, an area that could correspond with Karelia. "I look upon the Terra Feminarum as the hypothetical matrix of Northern pre-Christian—and likely more woman-positive—cultures," wrote Kaarina Kailo. "I see this Land as a convergence zone extending across Scandinavia, Finland, Samiland and the lands of Russian Finno-Ugric people."

Many centuries ago, the regions around what is now Finnish Karelia were populated by Finland's Indigenous Sámi people, who had a tradition of charismatic female shamans as the leaders of society. And in the folk epic *Kalevala*, which flowed from the cultural folk memories of earlier centuries, a northern land called Pohjola was ruled by a strong, feared female leader and shaman named Louhi, who engaged in struggles for the Sampo, the mythical mill of prosperity.

A few years ago, two researchers at the University of Helsinki, Risto Pulkkinen and Marko Salmenkivi, performed an analysis of place-names in geographic clusters in Finland as a way of exploring possible locations of the fabled Terra Feminarum. They were startled to find what Pulkkinen called a "very staggering" incidence of the word *Louhi* in and around North Karelia, especially in the area of Lake Pielinen, which is flanked by the mountain of Koli. "We concluded that in ancient times, Pohjola and Terra Feminarum might have been located in the Pielinen region," said Pulkkinen.

In other words, when I explored the hills and caves of Koli and walked on the shores of Lake Pielinen, I may have been traveling in precincts of the ancient Land of Women.

———————

FOR ME, WHAT started as a short-term family lark turned into an extended love affair with a Nordic nation, an accidental spiritual pilgrimage into an entirely different society, and a passage into a sisterhood that uplifted and enriched me.

After visiting and living in modern Finland and learning from its people and my long-lost Karelian sisters, I have come to believe that the mythical Sampo is not only a symbol for a mill that churns out gold and success, or a Holy Grail or a Golden Fleece, but it is also an insight.

It is an insight that can inspire and transform the world.

The insight is this—when a society strives to truly and humbly make each gender full partners in power and in leadership, from the halls of government to household affairs, and when the society deeply cares for and serves the welfare and well-being of all its people, and when its people respectfully engage with nature in their daily lives—the whole of society thrives.

The people of Finland are showing us that it can be done, and they are the first to acknowledge that the work is still in progress.

It is a reality that I've experienced with all my senses.

It is a reality that has fed my body and soul, in the heart of an enchanted forest.

The Sisterhood of the Enchanted Forest Recipes

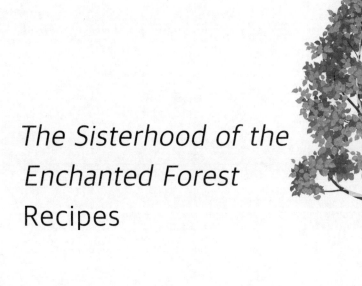

1. Marthas' Karelian Pies (three fillings)
2. Päivi's Brown Chanterelle Cookies
3. Maire's Lingonberry Porridge
4. Marthas' Chilled Bilberry (Blueberry) Soup
5. Marthas' Nettle Soup
6. Marthas' Summer Dandelion Salad
7. Marthas' Traditional Pan-Fried Perch
8. Marthas' Salmon Soup with Vegetables and Dill
9. Maija-Liisa's Lingonberry-Blueberry Multigrain Bread
10. Maija-Liisa's Spruce Sprout Syrup

Marthas' Karelian Pie Three Ways

The best place to taste one or more of these local snacks is Martat Café in the city center square in Joensuu in the warm months (*Marttakahvio ja piirakkapaja*, Kauppatori, 80100 Joensuu). The second best place, I must say, is your own kitchen. Here is the Martha Karelian pie recipe.

MAKES 20 PIES

Ingredients

Filling option 1: Rice
250 ml (1 cup) water
5.6 ounces porridge rice
750 ml milk, or plant-based milk (e.g., soy, oat, almond, etc.)
¼ teaspoon salt
1 egg

Filling option 2: Carrots
800 ml water
2.8 ounces rice
2.8 ounces chopped carrots
200 ml cream, 10 percent or 15 percent, or plant-based cream
¼ teaspoon salt
1 egg

Steps

First prepare the filling.

Preparation of filling option 1: Rice

1. Stir the rice in boiling water and cook for 10 minutes.

2. Add the milk and let the porridge simmer for 30 minutes, stirring along the bottom. Leave the filling to simmer with the lid on for less than 10 minutes.

3. Season the finished porridge with salt and cool it.

4. Stir the egg into the cooled porridge.

Preparation of filling options 2 and 3: Carrots or Beets

1. Stir the rice and carrots/beets into boiling water and cook for about 30 minutes, stirring occasionally.

2. Add cream and salt. Let the porridge simmer for about 10 minutes.

Filling option 3: Beets

800 ml water

2.8 ounces rice

2.8 ounces chopped beets

200 ml cream, 10 percent
   or 15 percent, or plant-
   based cream

¼ teaspoon salt

1 egg

Peel dough

150 ml water

1 tablespoon oil

¾ teaspoon salt

6 ounces rye flour

2 ounces wheat flour

For finishing: Melted butter,
   or vegetable oil and
   water

3. Pour the porridge into a flat container and pour a drop of cold water on top to prevent a crust from forming on the surface of the porridge.

4. Stir the egg into the chilled porridge.

To make pie shells:

1. Mix cold water, oil, salt, and flour with a wooden fork. Knead the dough smooth and firm.

2. Sprinkle the rye and wheat flour mixture on the table and place the dough over the flour. Divide the dough into twenty pieces.

3. Cover the divided dough pieces with a wet kitchen towel to prevent them from drying out.

4. Roll each dough piece with a rolling pin into thin round or oval shells. Place the shells on top of each other and sprinkle the rye flour in between. Cover the stack of shells with a wet kitchen towel. Fill the shells as soon as possible so that they do not stick together.

5. Take the crusts to the baking table, spread a spoonful of the filling in the middle of the crust (0.40 inches thick layer of filling) and leave a space of about 0.40 inches at the edges of the crust.

6. Turn the opposite edges over the filling and wrinkle the edges with your index fingers.

7. Transfer the pies to a baking sheet on baking paper.

8. Bake the pies at 525–570°F for about 15 minutes.

9. Brush the tops of the pies with melted butter/ vegetarian oil mixed with a drop of water.

10. Stack the hot pies in a bowl on top of each other and cover with baking paper and cloth.

Päivi's Brown Chanterelle Cookies

Päivi the Mushroom Queen took out a rectangle flat container from her car trunk in a parking lot outside of a café, where we met up. She said nothing and opened a lid. Inside, home-baked cookies were lined up neatly. She offered these cookies to Katja, Jenny, and me. We each took one and bit into it. Päivi then poured some black substance in a cup and offered it to us. "Chaga tea!" We were all ready for a foraging excursion.

MAKES 25 COOKIES

Ingredients

0.2 ounces dried brown
    chanterelles
2.6 ounces butter, or
    vegetarian alternative
1 egg
3½ tablespoons sugar
2.2 ounces oatmeal
1 tablespoon flour
½ teaspoon baking powder
Pinch of salt

Steps

1. Preheat the oven to 350°F.

2. Crush dried mushrooms into small pieces.

3. Melt butter, or vegetarian alternative.

4. Beat the egg and add to the butter.

5. In a mixing bowl, combine all the dry ingredients.

6. Add the mixed dry ingredients to the butter and egg mixture, and mix well.

7. Cover a baking sheet with a parchment paper.

8. Take a teaspoonful of cookie dough and place it on the baking sheet, and repeat until all the dough is used.

9. Bake the cookies at 350°F for 10 minutes.

10. Let the cookies cool on the baking tray, loosen, and remove them carefully.

11. Serve! (Store remaining cookies in an airtight container so the cookies stay crispy.)

Maire's Lingonberry Porridge

Finns eat lots of porridge for breakfast, desserts, and snacks. When children come home from school, they go straight to the fridge and serve themselves some porridge as an afternoon snack. It's a Finnish tradition. Martha member Maire had this homemade porridge waiting for her children in her fridge.

SERVES 4

Ingredients

1 quart water

1 pound 8 ounces lingonberries, or cranberries (fresh or frozen)

3.5 ounces semolina flour

2.8 ounces sugar (optional)

120 ml milk, or plant-based alternative

Steps

1. In a saucepan, boil the water.

2. Add the lingonberries to the boiling water, and simmer for about 10 minutes until the berries are cooked through.

3. Add the semolina and whisk to make it foamy.

4. Add sugar, if you are using.

5. Serve a ladleful of the porridge in a small bowl. Serve hot.

6. Let each diner drizzle milk and pinch of sugar.

7. Store in refrigerator for two to three days. After refrigerated, serve cold.

Marthas' Chilled Bilberry (Blueberry) Soup

By now almost everyone knows that berries are a superfood packed with antioxidants.

While I was chatting with my Finnish friends about dishes we could make with handpicked bilberries, chilled bilberry soup came up. I said, "I must try that!" I had never had a berry soup in my life. This makes a lovely breakfast, a snack, or even a desert during warm months.

SERVES 6

Ingredients

700 ml water
7 ounces bilberries
   (blueberries) (fresh or
   frozen)
1.7 ounces sugar

Thickener
2 tablespoons potato flour
100 ml water

Steps

1. Add water, bilberries, and sugar into a sauce pan. Bring the bilberry mixture to a boil on high heat, then reduce the heat to medium-high and continue to cook. Total cooking time is about 10 minutes.

2. Mix the potato flour with the 100 ml water to make a thickener.

3. Add the thickener to the bilberry soup, continuously pouring and mixing with a wooden fork or spatula.

4. Bring the soup back up to a boil, remove from the stove then let it cool to room temperature.

5. Sprinkle some sugar on the top to prevent it from crusting.

6. Chill in the fridge.

7. Serve chilled.

Marthas' Nettle Soup

On the very first Saturday in North Karelia, Helmi served hand-picked homemade nettle soup with the fish her husband, Matti, caught in the river below their house. Nettles are rich in antioxidants, vitamins C and A, calcium, and minerals.

SERVES 4

Ingredients

1.5 liters milk, or plant-based alternative

7 ounces boiled, minced nettles

3 tablespoons wheat flour mixed with a drop of water

1 teaspoon salt

1 teaspoon sugar

Steps

1. Boil the milk in a large saucepan.
2. Add the minced nettles and flour-water mixture to the boiled milk, let stew for couple of minutes.
3. Season the soup with the salt and pepper.
4. Serve hot.

USEFUL TIPS ON FORAGING, PREPARING, and Storing Nettles

For tips on foraging, preparing, and storing nettles, see this link from the Martha organization (in Finnish, but google translate is getting better at converting Finnish to English!): https://www.martat.fi/reseptit/nokkonen/

Marthas' Summer Dandelion Salad

IN SPRING, DANDELIONS POP UP and bloom in fields and grass patches throughout Finland. Pick young leaves with smooth edges, which taste mild, while grown leaves with zigzaggy edges are tough and bitter.

SERVES 4 AS SIDE SALAD

Ingredients

For the salad
2 pounds young, fresh, and
   tender dandelion leaves
2 pounds leafy greens
2 oranges or 1 grapefruit
2 small red onions or 1
   medium-sized yellow
   onion
4 dandelion flowers

For the dressing
4 tablespoons fresh orange
   juice
4 tablespoons fresh lemon
   juice
1 crushed garlic clove
¼ teaspoon dried herbs
   (onion, basil, thyme,
   marjoram, salt)
¼ teaspoon white pepper
1 tablespoon liquid honey

Steps

1. Pick some young dandelion leaves with smooth edges that have grown in a shaded place.
2. Rinse the dandelion leaves and tap them dry with kitchen paper or towel.
3. Cut/tear the leafy greens into bite sizes.
4. Peel the oranges/grapefruit and slice them.
5. Chop the onions.
6. Put all ingredients in to a salad bowl.
7. Blend the spices and honey with orange and lemon juice.
8. Pour the dressing on the salad and let rest for couple of minutes.
9. Garnish each serving with a dandelion flower.
10. Serve immediately.

Marthas' Traditional Pan-fried Perch

THIS IS A DISH HELMI and Matti served for brunch with the nettle soup (page 228) at their cabin-like house in the woods.

SERVES 4

Ingredients

1.3 pounds perch fillets
1 teaspoon salt
6 teaspoons butter, or
   plant-based oil
6 teaspoons vegetable oil
Black pepper
Chopped chives (optional
   topping)

Steps

1. Dry the perch fillets and season them with salt.

2. Heat a frying pan.

3. Heat 2 teaspoons of the butter and 2 teaspoons of the vegetable oil in the pan.

4. Fry the fillets in three portions in a butter-oil mixture in the frying pan for 2–3 minutes per side.

5. Wipe the pan clean between frying times.

6. Grind black pepper on the surface of fried fillets.

7. Garnish with the chives, and serve with vegetable dishes.

Marthas' Salmon Soup with Vegetables and Dill

This is a quintessential Finnish and Karelian dish. I enjoy it from a food stall in the town square, in a long-distance train café, a university cafeteria, and fine-dining restaurants.

The soup can also be prepared without milk, in which case you can increase the amount of fish broth. You can vary the soup with vegetables and spices.

SERVES 10

Ingredients

1.5 liters fish broth

Approximately 10 allspice berries

3.5 ounces onions

2.2 pounds potatoes

5.3 pounds leeks

10 ounces carrots

1.8 pounds salmon, cut into bite-size cubes

600 ml milk, or plant-based alternative

Chopped fresh dill

Pinch of salt

Pinch of black pepper

Steps

1. Boil the fish broth in a large saucepan.

2. Dice the onion; peel and slice the potatoes; cut the leeks in half lengthwise, wash, and then chop; and chop the carrots.

3. Add the vegetables to the boiling fish broth and cook for about fifteen minutes.

4. Add the salmon cubes and let the soup simmer until almost cooked through.

5. Add milk.

6. Bring to a boil and season the soup if necessary.

7. Serve hot with chopped fresh dill.

Maija-Liisa's Lingonberry-Blueberry Multigrain Bread

Ingredients

500 ml lukewarm water
2 ounces fresh yeast
1.7 ounces lingonberries
1.7 ounces blueberries
1 teaspoon salt
9 ounces white flour
9 ounces graham, spelt, or
   brown bread flour
1 ounce sunflower seeds
4 tablespoons vegetable
   oil

Steps

1. Dissolve the yeast in lukewarm water. Add the lingonberries and blueberries and oil to the yeast liquid.

2. In a medium-size bowl combine the salt, flours, and sunflower seeds.

3. Gradually add the dry ingredients to the liquid and work the dough until it is smooth and soft but not too wet.

4. Let the dough rise well under a kitchen towel (at least 30 minutes).

5. Preheat the oven to 390°F.

6. Pour the dough to tin/dish for baking bread and bake it in 390°F for 40 minutes or until baked through.

Maija-Liisa's Spruce Sprout Syrup

Ingredients

6 cups spruce sprouts
Water
2 pounds sugar
Lemon juice, or vanilla

Steps

1. Rinse sprouts and place them in a sauce pan.

2. Pour cold water just to cover the sprouds in the pan.

3. Let them soak overnight.

4. Boil sprouts in the same water for 2 hours and then sieve the mixture. At this point, there should be 1.5–2 liters of liquid.

5. Add sugar 1 pound per one liter of liquid, or some more or some less.

6. Boil the mixture for 2 hours, stirring all the time so it doesn't stick to the bottom. The longer you boil, the thicker syrup you'll get.

7. Season the syrup with lemon juice or vanilla.

8. Pour the hot syrup into heated jars and close the lids well.

9. When ready, the syrup is russet in color, and it can be served as dressing (e.g., for ice cream and berries) and as a garnish to game dishes.

Source Notes

Quotations are from author notes and interviews unless otherwise noted. Passages from the *Kalevala* are from the John Martin Crawford English translation published in 1888, available at http://www.gutenberg.org/files/5186/5186-h/5186-h.htm

"What is this fragrance around me?": Eino Leino, "Peace",
    translation by Lola Rogers, courtesy of Lola Rogers.
"Wide-spread they stand, the Northland's dusky forests":
    Andrew Barnett, *Sibelius* (Yale University Press, 2007),
    p. 321.
"Finland leads in UN Global Sustainable Development
    Comparison": YLE News, June 14, 2021. https://yle.fi
    /uutiset/osasto/news/finland_leads_in_un_global
    _sustainable_development_comparison/11981569

"The forest has been the mainstay of the life of all the Finnic peoples": Harald Haarmaan, *Modern Finland* (McFarland, 2016), p. 29.

"In the midst of winter, I finally learned": Albert Maquet, *Albert Camus: The Invincible Summer* (Humanities Press, 1972), p. 5.

"Some think the Finns are crazy": Haarmann, *Modern Finland*, p. 104. Finland's global rankings: See: https://www.good newsfinland.com/category/society/country-rankings/; https://www.stat.fi/tup/tilastokirjasto/itsenaisyyspai va-2019_en.html

"A forest people at heart": Deborah Swallow, *CultureShock! Finland: A Survival Guide to Customs and Etiquette* (Graphic Arts Center Publications, 2001), p. 61.

"Of course, Finland is not Utopia": Danny Dorling, Annika Koljonen, *Finntopia: What We Can Learn from the World's Happiest Country* (Agenda Publishing, 2020), p. xvi, 219.

"Finnish women are much more outgoing and approachable": "National Cultural Profiles—Finland", *The Guardian,* December 16, 2006, https://www.telegraph.co.uk/news /uknews/4205553/National-Cultural-Profiles-Finland.html

"The longest, straightest avenue, the Kirkkokatu": Hilary Finch, "From the Heart to the Finnish", *The Times* (UK), April 26, 1986.

"We know that, at its publication, the *Kalevala* was seen": Lotte Tarkka, *Dynamics of Tradition: Perspectives on Oral Poetry and Folk Belief; Essays in Honour of Anna-Leena Siikala on Her 60th Birthday* (Finnish Literature Society, 2003), p. 152.

"It was like discovering a wine-cellar filled with bottles of
    amazing wine": Tekijät Humphrey Carpenter, *J.R.R.
    Tolkien: A Biography* (Houghton Mifflin Harcourt, 2014),
    p. 67.

"When you humble yourself and admit": Tellervo Uljas,
    "Marianne Heikkilä: "I had a hard time admitting that I
    needed help", *eeva.com*, January 2017, https://www.apu.fi
    /artikkelit/marianne-heikkila-minun-oli-vaikea-myon
    taa-etta-tarvitsin-apua

"Stepping into a Finnish forest is something akin": Ali Noble,
    Sydney Morning Herald, "On the Road", April 23, 2005,
    https://www.smh.com.au/opinion/on-the-road-20050423
    -gdl6b2.html

Antipollution potential of mushrooms: see Shweta
    Kulshreshtha, Nupur Mathur, Pradeep Bhatnagar,
    "Mushroom as a Product and Their Role in
    Mycoremediation", *AMB Express*, April 2014, https://www
    .ncbi.nlm.nih.gov/pmc/articles/PMC4052754/

"He wished that the whole Valley had been empty": Tove
    Jansson, *Moominvalley in November* (Penguin UK, 2003),
    ebook.

"Chronic noise contributes to stress, annoyance": Lara S.
    Franco, Danielle F. Shanahan, Richard A. Fuller, "A
    Review of the Benefits of Nature Experiences: More Than
    Meets the Eye", *International Journal of Environmental
    Research and Public Health*, August 2017, https://www
    .ncbi.nlm.nih.gov/pmc/articles/PMC5580568/

Work of forest ecology professor Suzanne Simard and
    colleagues: see https://suzannesimard.com/research/

"Everything is connected, absolutely everything": Ferris Jabr,
    "The Social Life of Forests", the *New York Times Magazine*,
    December 2, 2020.
Research papers on forest bathing: Ye Wen, Qi Yan, Yangliu
    Pan, Xinren Gu, Yuanqiu Liu, "Medical Empirical
    Research on Forest Bathing (Shinrin-yoku): a Systematic
    Review", *Environmental Health and Preventive Medicine*,
    December 2019, https://pubmed.ncbi.nlm.nih.gov
    /31787069/; Marc Farrow, Kyle Washburn, "A Review of
    Field Experiments on the Effect of Forest Bathing on
    Anxiety and Heart Rate Variability," *Global Advances in
    Health and Medicine*, May 2019, https://www.ncbi.nlm.nih
    .gov/pmc/articles/PMC6540467/
"One of the mechanisms that facilitate": Marianna Pogosyan,
    "How Nature Heals: the Benefits of Forest Bathing",
    Psychology Today, November 19, 2020, https://www
    .psychologytoday.com/us/blog/between-cultures/202011
    /how-nature-heals
"What makes a sauna a venue for social events": Haarmann,
    Modern Finland, p. 97.
"There are few more quintessentially Finnish summer
    traditions": Petra Kaskonen, "Chasing Quiet Charm of
    a Finnish Summer: Scandinavian Country is a Place
    Where Silence is Celebrated", *National Post*, January 28,
    2016, https://nationalpost.com/travel/chasing-quiet
    -charm-of-a-finnish-summer-finland-is-a-place-where
    -simplicity-and-silence-are-celebrated
"In the sauna I relax physically and invigorate mentally":
    Innovation from Finland, Finnish government publication,

2017, https://finlandabroad.fi/documents/4248263/0
/100_Innovation_from_Finland+English+version
.pdf/7579ed39-5aa8-e21c-ef56-14b94da1b8d2?t
=1574776245356

Sauna bathing health benefits: Jari Laukkanen,
Tanjaniina Laukkanen, Setor Kunutsor,
"Cardiovascular and Other Health Benefits of Sauna
Bathing: A Review of the Evidence," *Mayo Clinic
Proceedings,* August 2018, https://pubmed.ncbi.nlm
.nih.gov/30077204/

"Kuopio almost dissolves into a tapestry": Leslie Li, "A Land of
a Thousand Lakes", *New York Times,* April 16, 1989, https
://www.nytimes.com/1989/04/16/travel/a-land-of-a
-thousand-lakes.html

"Finland may not have the geographical splendor of her
cousins": Matt Bolton, "Finland's Favorite Fruit",
News.com.au, July 19, 2012, https://www.news.com.au
/tablet/finlands-favourite-fruit/news-story/d4b114fd5b
6daef0557732f1088d3132

Berries linked to health benefits: for example, see
Aleksandra Kristo, Dorothy Klimis-Zacas, Angelos
Sikalidis, "Protective Role of Dietary Berries in Cancer",
Antioxidants (Basel), December 2016, https://www.ncbi
.nlm.nih.gov/pmc/articles/PMC5187535/

"Curses of the borderland": Emily Willingham, "Finland's
Bold Push to Change the Heart Health of a Nation",
Knowable, March 2018. https://knowablemagazine.org
/article/health-disease/2018/finlands-bold-push
-change-heart-health-nation

"The land is my source": Thomas A. DuBois, *Sacred to the Touch: Nordic and Baltic Religious Wood Carving* (University of Washington Press, 2017), p. 31.

"Each of the church's fourteen pews": ibid., p. 45.

"The same hunt provides food for men and women alike": Cornelius Tacitus, *Tacitus on Britain and Germany: A Translation of the Agricola and the Germania* (Penguin Books, 1965), p. 140.

"During the transition to the modern age": Andrew Soergel, "Minding the Nordic Inequality Gap", *U.S. News & World Report,* January 16, 2020, https://www.usnews.com/news /best-countries/articles/2020-01-16/gender-equality -perceptions-versus-reality-in-nordic-countries

"Finnish women's participation in the labor market"; "For me it feels like I won the lottery": Emma Graham-Harrison, "Feminism Comes of Age in Finland as Female Coalition Takes the Reins", *The Guardian,* December 14, 2019, https://www.theguardian.com/world/2019/dec/14 /feminism-finland-gender-equaity-sanna-marin

"Topelius declared Punkaharju as Finland's most beautiful landscape": https://www.kruunupuisto.fi/en/about-us /history/

2018 report by the Nordic Council of Ministers: Nordic Council of Ministers, "Leadership and Equal Opportunities at Work: The Nordic Gender Effect at Work," August 8, 2018.

Nima Sanandaji, "Cato Institute Policy Analysis: The Nordic Glass Ceiling," March 8, 2018, https://www.cato.org /sites/cato.org/files/pubs/pdf/pa-835.pdf

Some 47 percent of women and girls in Finland over fifteen
    experienced sexual or physical violence, in a third of the
    cases, the perpetrator is the victim's current or former
    partner: "Report: Women and Girls in Finland Still Face
    Violence, Poverty, Harassment", YLE News, October 3,
    2019, https://yle.fi/uutiset/osasto/news/report_women
    _and_girls_in_finland_still_face_violence_poverty
    _harassment/11004056

"This is a paradox: a high level of gender equality": Emma
    Graham-Harrison, "Feminism Comes of Age in Finland
    as Female Coalition Takes the Reins," *Guardian* (UK),
    December 14, 2019, https://www.theguardian.com
    /world/2019/dec/14/feminism-finland-gender-equality
    -sanna-marin

In 2016 survey, two thirds of people with disabilities reported
    having been discriminated against: "Survey: Two thirds
    of Disabled People Report Discrimination", YLE News,
    December 13, 2016, https://yle.fi/uutiset/osasto/news
    /survey_two_thirds_of_disabled_people_report
    _discrimination/9347929

2020 report from the Finnish government's Equality
    Ombudsman: https://syrjinta.fi/en/-/report-of-the-non
    -discrimination-ombudsman-racism-and-discrimina
    tion-everyday-experiences-for-people-of-african-descent
    -in-finland

"Sometimes foreign blood is a source of pride": Maryan
    Abdulkarim, "Somalian: A Column," YLE News, July 16,
    2019, https://yle.fi/uutiset/osasto/news/somalian_a
    _column_by_maryan_abdulkarim/10875708

Politico article: Maryan Abdulkarim, "Finland Is No Feminist
     Utopia," *Politico*, December 12, 2019, https://www
     .politico.eu/article/finland-is-no-feminist-utopia/
2018 report by the Nordic Council of Ministers and the
     Happiness Research Institute, "In the Shadow of
     Happiness," 2018, http://norden.diva-portal.org/smash
     /get/diva2:1236906/FULLTEXT02.pdf
"You almost feel like you don't have the right": "Suicide rates
     in Finland": Maddy Savage, "Being depressed in the
     'world's happiest country,'" BBC, September 25, 2019,
     https://www.bbc.com/worklife/article/20190924-being
     -depressed-in-the-worlds-happiest-country
World Economic Forum, "Global Gender Gap Report, 2021,"
     http://www3.weforum.org/docs/WEF_GGGR_2021.pdf
World Economic Forum, Social Mobility Index, https
     ://reports.weforum.org/social-mobility-report-2020
     /social-mobility-rankings/
Freedom House, "Freedom in the World Report," 2020, https
     ://freedomhouse.org/countries/freedom-world/scores
"Other than in this one conspicuous policy area, Finland's
     recognition of LGBTQ rights": Dorling and Koljonen,
     Finntopia, p. 209.
Partanen and Corson on Finland: Anu Partanen and Trevor
     Corson, "Finland is a Capitalist Paradise," *New York Times*,
     December 7, 2019, https://www.nytimes.com/2019/12/07
     /opinion/sunday/finland-socialism-capitalism.html
"We shall not cease from exploration": Sunil Kumar
     Sarker, *T.S. Eliot: Poetry, Plays and Prose* (Atlantic,
     2000), p. 154.

"The coolest hotel in New York City": Alex Fitzpatrick, Anne
    Most, and Joey Lautrup, "JFK's Iconic TWA Terminal Is
    Now the Coolest Hotel in New York City," *Time*, May 19,
    2019, https://time.com/5589561/twa-hotel-jfk/
"Grand Central of the Jet Age": Herbert Muschamp,
    "Architecture View; Stay of Execution for a Dazzling
    Airline Terminal," *New York Times*, November 6, 1994,
    https://www.nytimes.com/1994/11/06/arts
    /architecture-view-stay-of-execution-for-a-dazzling
    -airline-terminal.html
"The most dynamically modeled space of its era": Sarah
    Firshein, Preserving an Icon," *Curbed New York*,
    July 23, 2019, https://ny.curbed.com/2019/7/23/20696897
    /twa-hotel-jfk-airport-new-york-history-preservation
"The sexiest building on the planet": "Inside NYC's 'Mad
    Men'–Style Hotel with Gloriously Retro Rooms,
    FastCompany, February 21, 2019, https://www.facebook.
    com/FastCompany/videos/346702239269370
"Sweep us up and forward and into space": Eero Saarinen,
    Shaping the Future (Yale University Press, 2006), 24.
"Architecture is not just to fulfill man's need";
    "Architecture must make a strong emotional
    impact": Eero Saarinen, *Eero Saarinen on His Work:
    A Selection of Buildings Dating from 1947 to 1964 with
    Statements by the Architect* (Yale University Press,
    1968), 5, 10.
"Most original interior in decades"; "It is as if several
    architects were at work"; "As the passenger walked
    through the sequence"; "TWA is beginning to look

marvelous": *The TWA Terminal: The Building Block Series*
(Princeton Architectural Press, 1999), 3, 5.

"Express the drama and specialness and excitement"; "To the
extent that there was a golden age": Eric Wills, "Flights of
Fancy," *American Scholar*, June 3, 2019, https://the
americanscholar.org/flights-of-fancy/

"This hotel gave me nothing but feelings of pure joy":
Christopher Muther, "TWA Hotel Is a Time Machine to the
Glamorous World of Vintage Travel," *Boston Globe*,
January 9, 2020, https://www.bostonglobe.com/2020/01
/09/lifestyle/twa-hotel-is-time-machine-glamorous
-world-vintage-travel/

"Among all their marvels, trees are good listeners": Marianna
Pogosyan, "How Nature Heals: The Benefits of Forest
Bathing," *Psychology Today*, November 19, 2020, https
://www.psychologytoday.com/intl/blog/between-
cultures/202011/how-nature-heals?amp

Helsinki named the best city for families: https://www.hel.fi
/uutiset/en/helsinki/best-cities-for-families-in-2020
-revealed-helsinki-ranks-no1-out-of150#:~:text=Helsinki
%20has%20been%20named%20the,employment%20
rates%20and%20general%20affordability

Helsinki named best city for work-life balance: https://finland
.fi/life-society/helsinki-named-best-city-for-work
life-balance/

"There's a green crescent around Helsinki": Fiona Zublin,
"Could a City Park Be Your Grocery Store? In Finland,
Maybe," Ozy, June 13, 2018, https://www.ozy.com/around

-the-world/could-a-city-park-be-your-grocery
-store-in-finland-maybe/87030/

"You can put on a backpack in the courtyard": Ari
Turunen, "Helsinki, the World's Nature Capital,"
SLOW Finland, n.d., https://slowfinland.fi/en
/helsinki-the-worlds-nature-capital/

Pekka Kuusisto on Larin Paraske and Jean Sibelius:
"Sibelius's Roots: An Interview with Pekka Kuusisto &
Ilona Korhonen (Philharmonia Orchestra)," YouTube,
September 15, 2017, https://www.youtube.com/watch
?v=vC6d9jXK5Aw&t=320s

Halonen named most admired woman in YLE poll: Jenny
Timonen, "Yleisö äänesti: Tarja Halonen on inspiroivin
nainen—kärkikolmikkoon ylsivät myös Tove Jansson ja
Minna Canth," YLE News, March 8, 2021, https://yle.fi/aihe
/artikkeli/2021/03/08/yleiso-aanesti-tarja-halonen-on
-inspiroivin-nainen-karkikolmikkoon-ylsivat-myos

"The silence was the hardest": Daniel Reynolds, "Finland's
New Prime Minister Sanna Marin, 34, Was Raised by Two
Moms," *Advocate*, December 10, 2019, https://www
.advocate.com/world/2019/12/10/finlands-new-prime
-minister-sanna-marin-34-was-raised-two-moms

"Like many other Finns": Megha Mohan and Yousef Eldin,
"Sanna Marin: The Feminist PM Leading a Coalition of
Women," BBC News, November 24, 2020, https://www
.bbc.com/news/stories-55020994

"For me, human rights and equality of people"; "I joined
politics because I want to influence": Megan Specia, "Who

Is Sanna Marin, Finland's 34-year-old Prime Minister?"
New York Times, December 10, 2019, https://www.nytimes.
com/2019/12/10/world/europe/finland-sanna-marin.html

An "abundance" of love; "People have been saying it's the best
thing": Sheena McKenzie, "From Cashier to World's
Youngest PM: Finland's New Leader Breaks the Mold,"
CNN, December 23, 2019, https://edition.cnn.com/2019
/12/22/europe/finnish-prime-minister-sanna-marin
-profile-intl/index.html

"I'm extremely proud of Finland": "Sanna Marin: Estonia
Apologises after Minister Mocks Finland PM," BBC,
December 17, 2019, https://www.bbc.com/news/world
-europe-50818032

"Very happy that we now have a young female PM"; "I cannot
recall when politics last made me cry": Rachel Obordo,
"'The Country Faces a Bright Future': Finnish Readers
on Their New PM," *Guardian* (UK), December 10, 2019,
https://www.theguardian.com/world/2019/dec/10/the
-country-faces-a-bright-future-finland-readers-on-their
-new-pm

"A one-in-a-generation natural political talent"; "Her
performance at press conferences"; "Of course she is a role
model": Gordon Sander, "Premier for a Pandemic: How
Millennial Sanna Marin Won Finland's Approval,"
Christian Science Monitor, April 6, 2020, https://www
.csmonitor.com/World/Europe/2020/0406/Premier
-for-a-pandemic-How-millennial-Sanna-Marin-won
-Finland-s-approval

"Marin has smooth, pale skin": Rachel Donadio, "How a
    Millennial Prime Minister Is Leading Finland through
    Crisis," *Vogue*, April 1, 2020, https://www.vogue.com/article/
    millennial-prime-minister-leading-finland-through-crisis
"I feel that the American Dream can be achieved": Vicky
    McKeever, "Nordic Countries Are Better at Achieving the
    American Dream, Finland PM Sanna Marin Says," CNBC,
    February 4, 2020, https://www.cnbc.com/2020/02/04
    /sanna-marin-nordic-countries-best-embody-the-
    american-dream.html
"These countries are among those with the lowest numbers":
    Kenn Anthony Mendoza, "Meet Sanna Marin—
    Finland's Female Millennial Prime Minister, from an
    LGBT Family, Leading the War on Coronavirus," *South
    China Morning Post*, June 23, 2020, https://www.scmp.
    com/magazines/style/news-trends/article/3090246/
    meet-sanna-marin-finlands-female-millennial-prime
"There are countries led by men": Megha Mohan and
    Yousef Eldin, "Sanna Marin: The Feminist PM Leading
    a Coalition of Women," BBC News, November 24, 2020,
    https://www.bbc.com/news/stories-55020994
"Maybe it's not as big a deal in Finland": Lisa Abend,
    "Finland's Sanna Marin, the World's Youngest Female
    Head of Government, Wants Equality, Not Celebrity,"
    Time, January 17, 2020, https://time.com/collection/
    davos-2020/5764097/sanna-marin-finland-equality/
"Hopefully in the future it will be the new normal":
    Belinda Goldsmith, "Equality Won't Happen by

Itself, Says Finnish PM," Reuters, January 23, 2020, https://www.reuters.com/article/us-davos -meeting-women-idUSKBN1ZM1KR

"Finland arguably has the most popular": Gordon Sander, "Finland's President Can Hold His Own with Both Putin and Trump," *Foreign Policy*, September 10, 2020, https ://foreignpolicy.com/2020/09/10/finlands-president- niinisto-can-hold-his-own-putin-trump/

"Sanna Marin looked spectacular"; "Yesterday we said to each other I will": Annabel Sampson, "Prime Minister Sanna Marin Marries Her Partner of 16 Years," *Tatler*, August 3, 2020, https://www.tatler.com/article/finlands-prime- minister-sanna-marin-marries-markus-raikkonen

"I hope one day it won't be an issue"; "In every position I've ever been in"; "Finland is not a dream world": Sirin Kale, "'In Every Position I've Ever Been In, My Gender Has Always Been The Starting Point': Sanna Marin Opens Up About Sexism In Politics," *Vogue UK*, October 16, 2020, https://www.vogue.co.uk/arts-and-lifestyle/article /sanna-marin-finland-prime-minister-interview

"We all have to fight each and every day for equality": Vicky McKeever, "Finland's Sanna Marin Hopes Women Leaders Will Be the 'New Normal,'" CNBC, January 23, 2020, https://www.cnbc.com/2020/01/23/davos-2020- finland-pm-sanna-marin-discusses-gender-equality.html

"I want to build a society where every child": Sanna Marin (@ MarinSanna), Twitter, December 10, 2019.

"Financially responsible, socially equitable"; "The strength of a society is measured": "Prime Minister Sanna Marin's

New Year's Message, 31.12.2019," https://valtioneuvosto.fi
/en/-//10616/paaministeri-sanna-marinin-uudenvuoden
-tervehdys-31-12-2019

Kaarina Kailo on Terra Feminarum: conversation with Kaarina
Kailo based on her books *Finnish Goddess Mythology and the
Golden Woman: Climate Change, Earth-based Indigenous
Knowledge and the Gift,* see excerpt at: https://www
.magoism.net/2018/06/book-excerpt-1-finnish-goddess
-mythology-and-the-golden-woman-climate-change-earth
-based-indigenous-knowledge-and-the-gift-by-kaa
rina-kailo/ and Barbara Alice Mann & Kaarina Kailo, *Wo/
men who Marry Bears: The Antiquity and Spread of Maternal
Bear Spirituality,* in progress.

Finland and North Karelia as possible Terra Feminarum:
Janne Ahjopalo, "A Surprising Discovery in Folk Culture:
Women Ruled North Karelia?" YLE News, November 26,
2014, https://yle.fi/uutiset/3-7652321; Juha Pentikäinen,
Kalevala Mythology, Expanded Edition (Indiana
University Press, 1999), p. 172.

Acknowledgments

We thank Jessica Case, Mel Berger, Brendan Moriyama Doyle, Pasi Sahlberg, Helmi Järviluoma-Mäkelä, Matti Mäkelä, Katja and Tuomo Kolehmainen, Ambassador Charles Adams, Katherine and Joe Hooper, Shigeo and Chizuko Moriyama and the Moriyama families, Miki Wako, William and Marie Louise Doyle, Tiina Anola-Pukkila, Anu Brask, Juhamatti Eskiläinen, Anna Hakkarainen, President Tarja Halonen, Maria Havala-Napoles, Marianne Heikkilä, Risto and Tuula Helen, Saimi Hoyer, Petri and Anna-Leena Hukka, Ilona and Jari Huovinen, Tuomas Järvenpää, Maija-Liisa and Pekka Jeskanen, Sanna Jeskanen, Eeva Kainulainen, Helena Karhu, Eero Kilpi, Heidi Korpelainen, Ambassador Mika Koskinen, Cecilia Koskinen, Nina Kurth, Anita Lehikoinen, Päivi Leinonen, Gary and Irene Lincoff, Terhi Lindqvist, Eeva Mikkola, Jouni Mölsä, Terhi Mölsä, Jukka Monkonen, Irmeli Mustalahti, Ringa Nenonen, Erja, Tapio and Hertta

Nevalainen, Maija Pasanen, Kaarina Penninkilampi, Marjatta Pöllänen, Jaakko Puhakka, Sisko Räty, Harri and Sultana Rehnberg, Jaana Rehnström, Liisa Matveinen, Tom Selänniemi, Senni Timonen, Maarit Sallinen-Uusoksa, Jenny Salmela, Outi Savonlahti, Marja Simola, Riikka Simonen, Jessica LeTourneur Bax, Sirpa Rui, Liana Sutinen, Annika Suvivuo, Jarkko Tenhunen, Risto Turunen, Risto Pulkkinen, Liisa Tyrväinen, Riitta Uosukainen, Noora Vikman, Lola Rogers, Ambassador Manu and Mrs. Liisa Virtamo, Heikki Happonen, and Maire, Päivi and Raili Walling.

We are grateful to the Consulate General of Finland in New York, Finlandia Foundation National, the Fulbright Finland Foundation, the Martha Organization, Pohjois-Karjalan Martha, and the Regional Council of North Karelia (Pohjois-Karjalan Tulevaisuusrahasto).

Last but not least, we thank the people of Finland for their warm welcomes and friendship, and their wisdom and vision for building a better world.

About the Authors

NAOMI MORIYAMA grew up in Japan and moved to Manhattan in her twenties. She is a U.S.-Japan marketing professional and currently works for a leading fashion and beauty digital media company. She has coauthored three nonfiction books on traditional Japanese home-cooked meals and their health benefits with her husband William Doyle, and has been a judge on The Food Network's acclaimed *Iron Chef America*, and a featured guest on *The Today Show, The View,* and *Dr. Oz.*

WILLIAM DOYLE grew up in New York City and has produced TV programs for HBO, PBS, the History Channel, and A&E. Since 2015 he has served a Fulbright Scholar and scholar-in-residence at the University of Eastern Finland, as a Rockefeller Foundation Bellagio Center Resident Fellow, and as advisor to the Ministry of Education and Culture of Finland. His 2019 book *Let the Children Play* was coauthored with Pasi Sahlberg.